IMAGES
of England

TRING
1900-1950

It is impossible to think of Tring in the first part of the twentieth century without recalling the Rothschild family at Tring Park. As well as providing work for a large number of local people they took a benevolent interest in the town, contributing to a 'health service', building homes for working families, organising the Tring Show and providing money for many good causes. The most lasting reminder of the Rothschild family is the Tring Zoological Museum given to the second Lord Rothschild, Walter, as a coming-of-age present by his father, 'Natty'. It still attracts thousands of visitors a year. It was bequeathed to the nation in 1937. Older Tring people remember Lord Walter as a kindly white-bearded old gentleman presenting prizes and mementos to the children. This photograph from Miriam Rothschild's biography of Walter, *Dear Lord Rothschild*, shows him as a young man of twenty-four. At the time he was working as a banker but his lifelong passion was the building up of his unique museum.

IMAGES
of England

TRING
1900-1950

Jill Fowler

TEMPUS

In the early part of the century the Rothschild family played a considerable part in the lives of Tring people both as an employer and a benefactor. A similar position in New Mill was taken by the Mead family. They employed a large number of local people in their flour mill and also contributed generously to the New Mill community. Among other things Mr and Mrs W.N. Mead purchased a building, opened in 1922, to provide a new church, St George's, for those who did not wish to attend the Baptist church. In 1931 they gave New Mill a cricket pavilion. This early photograph shows the flour mill as seen from Mr and Mrs Mead's house. The large coat of arms, just behind the fountain, now decorates the front of the building on the Tringford Road.

First published 2003

Tempus Publishing Limited
The Mill, Brimscombe Port,
Stroud, Gloucestershire, GL5 2QG

British Library Cataloguing in Publication Data.
A catalogue record for this book is available from the British Library.

ISBN 0 7524 2685 0

Typesetting and origination by Tempus Publishing Limited
Printed in Great Britain by Midway Colour Print, Wiltshire

Contents

Introduction   7

Acknowledgements   8

1.   1900-1910   9

2.   1911-1920   33

3.   1921-1930   57

4.   1931-1940   79

5.   1941-1950   105

A wedding of great interest to local people took place on Thursday 2 April 1908 when Eveline Mary Grace married Mr Ernest John Rawlins at Akeman Street Baptist church. Both were from well-known Tring families. Miss Grace was the eldest daughter of Mr and Mrs Gilbert Grace of the long established ironmongers and hardware business in the High Street. Mr Grace, on the right in this photograph, was also chief of the fire brigade. Although in those days the engine was horse-drawn, he worked continuously to improve the equipment and efficiency of the service, trying constantly to reduce the time taken to get to the fire. Grace and Son is, of course, still in the High Street, with another Gilbert Grace in charge.

Introduction

When I first had the idea of producing a book on Tring, I saw it as a year-by-year record of the town from 1900 to 2000. I have since found that as I have collected photographs and information it would either end up as a very big, expensive book or a lot of the subject matter that would be of interest to local people would be left out. I have therefore started with the first fifty years, including 1900 as opinions differ as to when the century actually starts.

In 1900 Tring was mainly an agricultural town, very much under the influence of the immensely rich Rothschild family who lived in the Mansion in Tring Park and employed a large number of local people. Queen Victoria was still on the throne. The Boer War was still raging in South Africa, patriotically supported by Tring people, though not having much effect on their everyday lives. In the next fifty years there would be two world wars, having much more impact, including for many families the loss of loved ones and hardship at home.

Many of the photographs will not have been seen before, and appear here thanks to the generosity of Tring people who have lent their treasured family pictures. On a few occasions when an event was too important to leave out I have used a picture that may be familiar to some people. I realise that with this type of book I will be told that I have overlooked a certain person or event of importance to Tring, but I have tried to give a picture of life in the early years.

I am at present compiling material to illustrate the second half of the century and would be most grateful to hear local people's recollections of those years. I can be contacted at 19-20 Charles Street, Tring, Herts. HP23 6BD.

Acknowledgements

Joan Attryde, Wendy Austin, Lizzie Baldwin (née Drake), Doris Bardell, Hugh and Margaret Bass, Mike Bass, John Bly, Mervyn Bone, John Bowman, Barbara Buckley, *The Bucks Herald*, Dennis Burch, Rosemary Butler, Connie Carter, the Catholic Church of St Francis de Sales, Margaret Crabtree, Clive Dobbs, Laurie Fowler, Dudley Fulks, Steve Gates, Mabel Goodliffe, Frank Gower, Bob Grace, Gilbert and Julie Grace, Gary Harrop, Jeff Hawkins, Bill Hearn, the High Street Baptist Church, Josie Jordan, David Kempster, Phyllis King (née Killick), Joan and Arthur Kitchener, Vera McKernan, Doris Miller, Rita Mitchell (née Horne), Pat Moss-Carlsson, Muriel Orton, George and Dorothy Prentice, Gus Proctor, Josie and Alan Rance, Stan Rance, Ann Reed, Dena and Doug Reeve, David Ridgewall, Miriam Rothschild, Frank and Janie Standen, Rose and Doug Sinclair, Kathleen Stevens, Elsie Thompson (née Tugby), Tring British Legion, Tring Town Council, Tring Park Cricket Club, Tring 1st Scout Group, Frank and Barbara Thorn, Ron and Aileen Wheeler, Jimmy Wood.

One
1900-1910

In 1900 the Old Market House that had stood in front of the church since the seventeenth century was demolished and the new Market House built on the corner of Akeman Street. This very old photograph shows the old one opposite the old Rose and Crown that stood at that time level with the other buildings on the road. Records date back to 1650 and describe a corn loft over the market house and in 1819 it was said that underneath was a pillory and a cage, a temporary lock-up for any Tring person the worse for drink. The two shops beyond were also knocked down, giving a clear view of the church.

Demolition started in July 1900 and proceeded through the summer. In August when plaster was removed from the front the initials 'H.G.' and the date '1680' were found carved on a post. This was for Henry Guy (1631-1710) who became Lord of the Manor of Tring and had the mansion built in Tring Park from a design by Christopher Wren. In October a large iron hook mounted on a long pole was uncovered and was believed to have been used to pull down burning buildings to prevent the fire from spreading. It was preserved and moved to the new Market House and still survives.

The New Market House, designed by William Huckvale, Lord Rothschild's architect, was built on the site of Mr Mead's house, butchers shop and slaughterhouse. It was opened by Lord Rothschild on Friday 13 July 1900. The Market House was paid for by public subscription as a memorial to Queen Victoria's Diamond Jubilee and had the ground floor open for traders' stalls. The police station beyond had yet to be built.

At the beginning of 1901 Thomas Grace announced that he was handing over his corn and seed business at the maltings in Akeman Street to his son Frank Grace. Generations of the Grace family had run the business on the same premises and Frank's son, Bob, carried on from him. It is now a group of individual homes known as 'Graces Maltings'. This portrait of Mr Grace is by Payne of Aylesbury who had a studio in Tring.

On 22 January 1901 Queen Victoria died. There was genuine sorrow in Tring: flags were flown at half mast, blinds were drawn and prayers were said in the churches. Ten men from the Tring Volunteers F Company under Major Jenney went to Windsor as part of the guard at the Queen's funeral. Later, in April, a Mr Alexis Krouss came to the Victoria Hall to give a lantern lecture to a most appreciative audience on the life and reign of Queen Victoria. This picture is from a coloured photograph printed on silk.

On 4 February 1901 the chairman of the Urban District Council, Mr Butcher, read the proclamation of the accession of His Majesty King Edward VII. A platform was built under the Market House for the occasion, the Tring Volunteers formed a guard of honour and a crowd of Tring people assembled to watch. With Mr Butcher were the Revd S. Tidswell, vicar of Tring, Mr J.G. Williams of Pendley Manor and Mr A.W. Vaisey, clerk of the council. Later the bells of Tring church were rung unmuffled for the first time since the Queen's death.

In May 1901 it was announced that the Victoria Hall and the adjoining premises had been sold and were to be used as a factory. This saddened many local people; it was described as 'one of the finest halls for miles around', but it was felt that it could not be a bad idea if it provided work for Tring people. For some time it became 'Victoria Works', the factory producing mineral water, cider, jam and pickles. It is thought that some public use was made of the upstairs hall and in 1906 the papers started to report comedy shows, skating exhibitions, picture shows and Church Lads' Brigade events held there. The pickle factory seems not to have existed for very long, though this photograph taken early in the century shows the hall clearly marked 'Victoria Works'.

A directory of 1890 said that the Victoria Hall was erected in 1886 on the site of the former assembly room built in 1825. It was designed by William Huckvale, Lord Rothschild's architect. It was the British Legion's headquarters for many years, at the invitation of Lord Rothschild, although their tenancy was ended in rather unfortunate circumstances. Before premises were purpose built in the High Street, the Victoria Hall housed the Tring public library. As can be seen from the photograph, the big hall could be used for some quite impressive banquets; in this case the tables are laid for a New Year party for local children put on by the British Legion.

King Edward VII was crowned on 26 July 1902. He was popular in Tring, being a frequent visitor to the town as a guest of Lord Rothschild when he was Prince of Wales. On the day, the children were given coronation medals and assembled in the Green Man meadow, now the main Tring car park, to form a procession to walk to Tring Park. There were roundabouts, switchbacks, swings and Punch and Judy shows, and several bands were there to entertain. Later the children sat down to tea and the day ended with a bonfire and fireworks.

On 20 August 1902 the *Sketch* newspaper, which was publishing a series called 'Beautiful homes and their owners' produced, as the eleventh in the series, a two-page article on Lord Rothschild's mansion in Tring Park. Mr J.T. Newman of Berkhamsted was asked to take the photographs. Mr Newman was a well-known local photographer and produced many of the early postcards of the area. His photograph of the South Front, seen here, was later a popular postcard. Other views were the London Lodge, the shrubbery and rheas (American ostriches) in the park.

On 17 December 1902 a banquet was held in the Victoria Hall for the soldiers who had returned from the Boer War which had ended on 31 May that year. The Herts Cider and Preserve Company offered the use of the hall for the occasion and the Rose and Crown Hotel provided the catering. Eighteen soldiers were given a silver souvenir watch inscribed inside with the name of the recipient. At least one of these watches survives today. They were presented by the Rt Hon. Lord Chesham on behalf of the town of Tring. Pictured here is Trooper Arthur Francis Wright who was one of the Boer War volunteers to receive a watch. Trooper Wright also served in the First World War, as a sergeant in the ASC. He was fortunate to survive both wars. More remarkable was the survival of his son, Ernest, who in the Second World War was torpedoed three times while serving in the Merchant Navy. On the second occasion in 1943 he and his shipmates were in a leaking lifeboat in the South Atlantic when the commander of the German U-boat picked them up, made the lifeboat serviceable, gave them cigarettes and set them adrift. Five days later they were picked up by an Allied merchant ship. The following year his next ship was also torpedoed, this time fortunately nearer to land.

In September 1902 it was decided that the exterior woodwork on St Martha's church in Park Road needed to be restored. The church closed on 14 September. A lady who preferred to remain anonymous raised the £40 needed for the restoration by a local collection and the work was finished in time for the harvest festival on 6 October. This photograph, taken early in the twentieth century, is by Cyril Howlett, who lived at the post office stores in King Street and later became the postmaster. It was not until the gales of 1987 removed the last of the trees that St Martha's could be seen as clearly as it can today.

For many years in the first part of the century the Hon. Walter Rothschild, the founder of Tring Museum, kept exotic animals in Tring Park, including wallabies – similar to kangaroos but smaller. In March 1903 a London newspaper referred to eight 'kangaroos' packed in specially made crates for dispatch by Walter to the London Docks. On Euston station a crate was damaged and one of the animals escaped. After a considerable chase, to the amusement of train passengers, the poor creature was captured and continued its journey, though it was said to be slightly injured.

Early in 1903 the council discussed the introduction of a new spray for the water cart to lay the dust in the High Street on hot summer days. Shopkeepers had long been complaining about dust on their wares that in those days would be displayed outside their shops. The surveyor went to see a patent spray at work but did not think it was suitable for Tring's flint roads. Instructions were given to Mr Grace of the High Street ironmongers to make a suitable spray for their cart. Mr Grace did not entirely agree with the design but said that if his modified model did not meet their requirements he would present it to the council free of charge. If it did, he would like to be paid by August.

Although the new spray used about three times more water, it was obviously satisfactory as it was in use for many years until more modern surfaces on roads reduced the problem of dust. The High Street photograph shows the water cart in action. On very hot days the children would run along behind, getting sprayed with water to cool them down. The other photograph shows the water cart being filled from the standpipe at the corner of Charles Street.

Mr John Woodman, the landlord of the Green Man inn for about thirty years, died in January 1903. The next month Messrs W. Brown and Co. held an auction there and it was said that various lots commanded very good prices. The inn belonged to the Tring Park Estate and Lord Rothschild decided to demolish it. This old photograph, although a very informal one, shows the ivy-covered Green Man inn with its buildings beyond. It stood opposite the old forge, where the entrance to the memorial gardens is now. For many years the Green Man Meadow, next to the forge, now the site of the car park, was used for fairs and circuses. In the distance can be seen the wall that still exists. Originally built round Lord Rothschild's water gardens, it has recently been lowered to give a more open aspect to the memorial gardens.

This photograph is taken from a postcard issued early in the century. It can be seen that the Green Man was a substantial building considered worthy of being the subject of a postcard. Records show that John Philby brewed there in 1846 and John Woodman from 1878 to 1895. It was a popular meeting place for local clubs and societies. On 20 May 1887 Mr Woodman charged the Tring Association for the Prosecution of Felons £4 for twenty dinners. By 23 May 1892 the price for the dinners was exactly the same but 2s 6d had been added to the bill for a committee room. Mr Woodman appears to have been quite an easy-going man as both bills were not settled until well into the following August.

On the night of Wednesday 6 May 1903 a serious fire broke out in the electric machinery shop at the Bulbourne Works of the Grand Junction Canal Company. At about midnight the news was sent to Tring. The messenger from Bulbourne went by bicycle and on reaching the High Street after midnight was stopped by the police sergeant on duty. He was too breathless to explain his mission but after a short while recovered sufficiently to speak and was allowed on his way.

On hearing of the news of the fire at the Bulbourne Works the Tring fire brigade with their captain, Gilbert Grace, hurried to the scene. In those days the fire engine was drawn by horses which had to be caught and harnessed. The horses used would often be those of Mr John Gower, who had a removals business in Queen Street, and usually Mr Gower would drive them himself. It took the fire brigade two to three hours to get the fire under control. They were unable to save the building but the machinery was virtually undamaged.

Tring is surrounded by canals and reservoirs and in the early days a great deal of trade involved goods transported by barges on the canal. At the beginning of each year the surveyor made a report to Tring Council, as an inspector under the Canal Boats Act, to describe conditions on the canal. In January 1904 forty boats were registered and there were thirty-eight men, twenty-one women and forty-six children under twelve years old living in them. Life could be hard for the boat people and in the severe winters the barges could be locked in the ice for weeks, the icebreakers not always being able to release them. When they were unable to earn a living the bargees and their families suffered considerable hardship. Nowadays the canals are used for recreational purposes and the gaily-painted boats can still be seen travelling the waterways.

This photograph, taken at about the same time in nearby Berkhamsted, shows the boat people in their typical clothes of the day. Their barge is just going through the lock.

In late August 1904 a sad accident happened in Tring High Street. Young Nellie Thorn, daughter of Jesse Thorn, licensee of the Rose and Crown Hotel, rode her bicycle from Mr Dawe's yard, nearby, and was unable to stop. The station bus was going by at the time and one of the wheels went over her leg which was badly broken. A Tring doctor, Dr Brown, set the leg and she obviously recovered as she lived to reach her seventieth birthday in 1964. The photograph shows Nellie, on the left, outside the Rose and Crown with her family. Her father Jesse stands with his dogs at the other end of the group.

The family of Jesse and Mary Ann Thorn. The children at the back are Nellie and Harry. The little girl at the front is Edith and Doris and Frank stand either side of their mother. This well-posed photograph, taken by Mr and Mrs S.G. Payne and Son of Aylesbury, Thame and Tring, would suggest that to be a landlord of Tring's largest hotel was a position of some prestige and he could provide comfortably for his wife and family. Jesse's father Jabez had been landlord of the Rose and Crown before him.

In May 1904 a meeting was held in the Market House to consider the formation of a camera club. Although amateur photography did not enjoy the widespread popularity it does now, there were several very keen photographers in the town and a lot of excellent photographs taken then survive to this day. Herbert Grange of Tring Grove, who had recently been on a photographic tour of Canada, was largely responsible for the foundation of the Tring and District Camera Club. The Hon. Charles Rothschild, himself a keen photographer, was elected president and Mr Grange vice-president. Frank Grace, pictured here, was the treasurer and the committee included William H. Huckvale, son of the well known Tring architect. Mr Grace's photographs and lantern slides have given a wonderful picture of life in Tring over the years.

At the end of November the Camera Club held its first exhibition. Medals were awarded in a dozen classes and although they were open to amateurs and professionals alike, it was recorded that a professional photographer only won one reserve. Mr Huckvale did well in the competition, securing several medals, one of them, the smallest pictured here, being won in 1904. The larger medal was won by Mr Huckvale in 1906. Although the Tring Camera Club was discontinued, perhaps because of the war, it was revived in the 1960s and continues to this day.

At the beginning of 1905 the Rose and Crown Hotel was still level with the other buildings in the High Street. It was an old coaching inn and the coach Good Intent left from here daily for Aylesbury. Although the frontage gave the impression that it was a large building it had very little depth and Lord Rothschild, who had come to Tring in 1872, decided that it should be replaced by a larger hotel. It was not big enough to accommodate his numerous guests who came to Tring. Plans for the new hotel, by his architect, William Huckvale, were passed in early January. Again the photograph shows the landlord, Jesse Thorn, and his wife by the entrance.

Work was soon started to prepare for the new hotel. First the three shops beyond the old Rose and Crown were demolished, as the photograph shows. They were Nos 14, 15 and 16 High Street and housed the businesses of Jesse Wright the butcher, Henry Stevens, a wholesale boot and shoemaker, and Edward Craddock Knight, a decorator, gas fitter and plumber. Henry Stevens moved to Chesham and founded a boot factory there. It was agreed that the old hotel would not be demolished until the new Rose and Crown was completed, to avoid loss of trade, thus later providing a large forecourt for vehicles to pull in on arrival.

In 1906 Tring's oldest inhabitant was James Stevens. A keen churchman, he regularly attended the parish church. On his way on a Sunday in January he slipped and fell near Frogmore Street. PC Simpkins, on duty nearby, helped him into Mr Jeffery's shop opposite and a bath chair was fetched and he was wheeled home. He was well enough to get up to celebrate his ninety-eighth birthday the following Tuesday and he lived to be 103. The photograph shows Mr Stevens in the smocked 'frock' that he usually wore.

By 1906 the new Rose and Crown had been built and the old hotel demolished. On its completion it was made over by Lord Rothschild to the Hertfordshire Public House Trust, forerunner of Trust House Forte. It became a gathering place for the Tring Cycling Club before and after their excursions into the countryside; and as many as fifty motor cars would start from the Rose and Crown when competing in the hill-climbing tests at Dancers End. In those days there was access through the centre of the building to the large yard behind.

In the early part of the century tradesmen in Tring were well known and respected by all the local people. The wedding of Edith Maud Grace to Robert Warrior brought together two of the best-known families in the town. It was celebrated on Wednesday 14 March 1906. Miss Grace's late father had his bakery business at 89-90 Akeman Street, the shop being Warriors for many years. The bride was given away by her brother, Frank, and the two bridesmaids were her sisters, Ethel and Lilian. The ceremony at the parish church was performed by the Revd H. Francis who had succeeded the Revd S.W. Tidswell in 1903. Mr and Mrs Warrior's daughter, Mabel, was a keen performer with the Tring Amateur Operatic and Dramatic Society as a girl and as Mrs Goodliffe was well known and popular in the town.

Early in 1907 Lord Rothschild's younger son, the Hon. Charles Rothschild, married a Hungarian lady, Roszika von Wertheimstein. Although the marriage took place in Vienna, Tring celebrated the occasion, the church bells rang and the Tring Park Estate employees were given a day's holiday. When the young couple visited Tring after a honeymoon in Venice, everywhere was decorated to welcome them. Over the gates to Tring Park the words spelled out a welcome in Hungarian. Charles and Roszika's son, Victor, later inherited the title and properties in Tring after the death of his uncle, Walter Rothschild.

Until 1883 Long Marston people worshipped at the little church of All Saints, which dated back to the twelfth century with a fifteenth-century tower. It had already been said that the church was beyond repair and a new church was built just across the road from the Vicarage that had been built in 1873. Only the tower from the old church was preserved and in 1966 it was scheduled as an ancient monument. Recently local enthusiasts have raised money to restore the old tower.

The building of the new church was carried out by Mr H. Fincher of Tring and was consecrated on 31 July 1883. A tower was included in the plan but was not in fact added. However, by 1907, due to subsidence, it was found that considerable restoration was required. The worshippers at Tring churches helped the people of Long Marston to raise the money, just over £1,000, that was needed. This time the work was done by a local man, Job Gregory, and was completed in 1907, and included the addition of heavy buttresses. The following year a porch and vestry were added as a memorial to Mr Gregory.

In March 1907, Thomas Seeley Green MRCVS, a veterinary surgeon, started his business at the Brewery House in the High Street. Here he is seen competing at the Tring Show in Tring Park. The Tring Show, generously supported by Lord Rothschild, was said to be the largest one-day show in the country and was eagerly looked forward to by local people. It was held in early August.

Early the following year Mr Seeley Green was driving a tandem past the sewerage operations in Langdon Street, pictured here, when the leading horse slipped into the trench, dragging the other one with it. The hole was said to be about ten feet deep but this was perhaps a slight exaggeration. Two men were working in the trench at the time and they were got out with some difficulty, one said to be hurt. Getting the horses out was even more difficult and by then a large crowed had gathered. Mr Seeley Green was not injured, and it was not recorded whether the horses suffered any injury.

On 1 June 1908 there was a serious railway accident at Tring station, said to have been caused by wrongly set points. Twenty-seven coal trucks that had come from Nuneaton should have gone into a siding but went instead into the coal yard, crashing into about eighteen wagons that were already there. A seventeen-year-old boy named Higby, from Harrow Yard in Akeman Street, was crushed and killed instantly. Another lad named Butler was injured and was said by Dr O'Keefe who attended the accident to be suffering from shock. Soon to arrive on the scene was Police Sergeant Baldock from Tring, in response to a telegraph message from the stationmaster. The boy holding the shovel is Sidney Gower.

On Wednesday 12 July 1908 the Akeman Street Baptist church celebrated the centenary of the erection of a place of worship on the site of the present chapel. In 1808 a smaller church was built there with Mr Seymour as the first minister. In 1813 Mr Glover was appointed pastor and enjoyed such a long ministry that local people would refer to it as 'Glover's chapel'. In 1832 the foundation stone of the present Akeman Street chapel was laid and a building 51ft square and capable of seating 700 people was erected, and it has been altered very little to this day. The thanksgiving service to celebrate the centenary was held by Pastor L.H. Colls. This photograph was taken from the north side.

Saturday 14 February 1909 was an important day for Wigginton. Winifred Ada Marc, daughter of Alexander Marc of Champneys, married German-born Heinrich Roever of Osterode, in the Hertz Mountains. The wedding took place at Wigginton church. The village was decorated with coloured poles and bunting and at each end a leafy arch was built with a sign above it. This photograph shows what the bride would have seen as she entered the village, 'Long life and happiness'. At the other end near the school the motto was 'Not two, but one, while life shall run'. The photograph was taken by Mr J.T. Newman of Berkhamsted.

Later in November 1909 the death occurred of one of the town's best-known residents, John Tripp Clement, who passed peacefully away at the age of eighty. He was the son of John Clement and his mother was a daughter of Mr Tripp of The Grove, Tring. Like his father and grandfather he carried on the long-established business of watchmaker and jeweller in the High Street. The shop was one of those that were later demolished to make the entrance to Dolphin Square. Born in 1829, Mr Clement was not only a very popular businessman but also a very enthusiastic local historian. He carefully recorded local events and collected newspaper cuttings, making an important contribution to the records of Tring. This photograph was taken through the entrance to Tring Brewery.

Elsie Mary Maull, seen here with her dogs Smut and Billy, was born at Prospect House Boys' School, which stood on the corner of Park Road and the Chesham Road, when her father was headmaster. Her sister, Jessie E. Maull, married Harry Foster Young, the grandson of the late Mark Young who had been principal of the school before Mr Maull. Elsie was her bridesmaid. In 1909 Lord Rothschild decided that the school must go, as he chose to clear the area and continue his grounds along the southern edge of Tring. In spite of his vast financial superiority it was said that he was not able to close Chesham Road after having the school demolished. Mr Maull moved his school to Brookfield in Brook Street. Elsie had been on the teaching staff at Prospect House as a music teacher. In 1909 she decided not to go to Brook Street but to give private piano lessons at her home, Westholme, on Western Road. Over the years she had many successful pupils. She lived in Tring all her life and died in 1946 at the age of sixty-nine. In the background of this photograph can be seen the Duckmore Lane allotments and the Aylesbury Road.

In August 1910 tenders were sent to the council for converting the lower part of the Market House into a station for the fire brigade. The estimate of £130 from the local builders, J. Honour and Sons, was accepted. The work was finished by October. Large folding doors were fitted to the front to make access easier and the fire engine was housed there until the purpose-built station was built in Brook Street in 1969. By then the Market House was not big enough for modern fire engines. This photograph was taken some years after the conversion as the police station beyond was not built until 1913.

In 1910 the L & NW Railway company, wishing to improve the appearance of their stations, offered a sum of money to help stationmasters make their stations more attractive. Mr Bradley, the stationmaster of Tring was enthusiastic and drew up a scheme for beautifying three platforms, in all about a mile in length. It was said at the time that the bright and attractive appearance of the platforms was a matter of general congratulation. This photograph taken some time later shows that the flower beds at Tring station were still being lovingly cared for.

Two
1911-1920

In Aston Clinton, just a short way from Tring, another branch of the Rothschild family lived in the local mansion, Aston Clinton Park. When Louisa, Lady de Rothschild, died in 1910 the people of Aston Clinton and Buckland contributed to the cost of a drinking fountain to be erected in her memory. It was completed the next year and in May was unveiled by two of the oldest of the late Lady Rothschild's employees, Mr James Rolf and Mr Richard Morris. Speeches were made and the drinking fountain trough, not visible in this photograph, was filled with water. It still remains at the side of the road as you go through Aston Clinton but sadly a large piece of the top has recently been removed by vandals. They probably had no knowledge of the lady to whom it was dedicated, nor the good work she had done in her lifetime to improve conditions for local people.

In the spring of 1911 another interesting wedding took place at the Akeman Street Baptist church, with the Revd L.H. Colls officiating. Alma Dorothea Wright, daughter of Albert E. Wright of the well-known firm of G. Wright and Sons, butchers, married Arthur James Bagnall, son of James Bagnall. In those days the names of the mothers of the bride and bridegroom were usually not included in the description of the wedding. Both Mr Bagnalls were tailors and also deputy registrars of births, deaths and marriages. Many older people remember going to No. 1 Albert Street to have clothes made or altered. The photograph shows Mr and Mrs Bagnall in the back garden of their home soon after their marriage.

By 1911 the Hon. Walter Rothschild's museum in Akeman Street, built in 1889, was much too small to house his growing collection of birds, animals and insects. The new extension, built that year, was attached to the old one and formed three sides of a square, looking much as it does today. As well as space for exhibits, workrooms and a study for Walter there was a large basement for storing reserved specimens, packing cases etc. Now part of the British Natural History Museum, Tring Museum is as popular with visitors as it was in the early part of the last century.

On Thursday 4 May 1911 New Mill lost a familiar landmark when Mr W.N. Mead of Tring Flour Mills demolished his old windmill. He needed the ground to extend the steam-powered mills then in use. The lower brickwork was carefully replaced by wooden struts and when it was ready a steel cable and winch pulled them out, ensuring it fell in the right direction. Mr Mead obviously arranged for a photographer to be at the scene as a sequence of pictures exist covering the event. Tring still has a windmill, Goldfield Mill, minus its sails, at the top of Miswell Lane. It is now a private house.

An earlier photograph of the mill at New Mill when it was still in use.

In the autumn of 1912 Gilbert Grace, the captain of Tring fire brigade, decided that it was time for him to retire. He had been captain for many years and it was largely his enthusiasm that kept the brigade together in the days when the firemen were all volunteers and had other demands on their time. Mr Grace was, of course, best known in the town as a businessman and a very forward-thinking engineer. G. Grace and Son at this time were manufacturing ironmongers and many of the local examples of beautiful wrought ironwork were designed by him and made in his workshop. Here he is standing by a set of gates leading to the mansion garden. When Gilbert Grace died in 1914 at the age of sixty, his loss was keenly felt in the town. His son, Gilbert Charles Grace, carried on the business started by his predecessors 164 years before. It is still an asset to Tring shoppers today and the workshops are used for classic car repairs.

In 1912 Lord Rothschild decided to build a row of cottages on the west side of Brook Street just past the Silk Mill. The trees shown here were felled and preparations made but it was found that the ground was quite unsuitable as it soon became waterlogged. It was therefore decided to build eight cottages on the bank on the opposite side of the road. These houses still stand overlooking the town with their long gardens sloping down to Brook Street. The ground round the brook, known as 'The Feeder', has recently been landscaped and makes a pleasant walk between New Mill and Tring. The photograph shows the bank opposite where the cottages were built and beyond it the Tring gas works.

In 1912 many Catholics in Tring worshipped at a church in Berkhamsted. Mass was celebrated once a month in the Victoria Hall. In April 1912 a start was made on the Roman Catholic church in Langdon Street. At first a temporary iron structure was contemplated but Father Henry Hardy, who was credited with building churches in several other towns, arranged for it to be a permanent brick building. It would hold about fifty people, plenty of room for the worshippers at the time. The first public service was held on Sunday 18 August 1912. By the 1990s the space was completely inadequate and in 1992 Father McGuinness suggested that the church needed to be considerably enlarged. Unfortunately he became ill and died the following year; but later Father Tony Potter took up the project again and in November 1999 the greatly enlarged church of Corpus Christi was re-opened. The photograph shows the church before it was enlarged, but after the porch and tower were added in the 1960s and the bell turret on the main building removed.

In the early part of the century women were demanding the vote. Suffragette headquarters opened in London in 1912. In 1913 Sylvia Pankhurst was arrested for hurling a piece of concrete at a painting, shattering the glass. It was said that this was modest by Suffragette standards; many paintings had been hacked in Manchester Art Gallery and several stately homes burnt to the ground. This may have been an exaggeration but Tring took no chances. The vicar, the Revd H. Francis, announced that Tring church would be locked at all times unless a service was being conducted as churches all over the country were being damaged. In February 1913 Winston Churchill, who was then the First Lord of the Admiralty, was invited to a large house party with Lord Rothschild at Tring Park for the weekend. Mr Churchill was known to have little sympathy with women who wanted the right to vote and it was thought the 'Militant Suffragettes' would make an unwelcome appearance. All the entrances to the park were closely guarded by uniformed police and some in plain clothes assisted them. However they had a quiet weekend and Mr Churchill left Tring on Monday morning.

In the summer of 1913 the Revd L.H. Colls decided that the time had come for him to leave the Akeman Street Baptist church and accept an invitation to a church in St John's Wood in London. He had been there for eighteen years and his Tring parishioners were sorry to see him go. At a farewell gathering in September he was presented with gifts and speeches were made by various local dignitaries, including the Revd C. Pearce from the United Free church in the High Street and the Revd T. Percy George from the New Mill Baptist church.

In September of 1913 the new purpose-built police station was completed in the space beyond the Market House. It had been hidden from view by a hoarding and when it was removed the new building was received with mixed reactions. It was described as a severe and business-like building doubtless admirably adapted for the purpose for which it was erected. It was felt, however, that it hardly added to the beauty of the High Street and did not harmonise with the buildings on either side. Someone even said that perhaps the council did not want to make it too attractive. The police station still stands there, used for the purpose for which it was built, and has long been accepted as part of Tring High Street.

The year 1914 started on a sad note in the Akeman Street Baptist church, when Thomas Glover died on 9 January. Mr Glover was born in Tring on 1 December 1822 and was pastor of the Akeman Street church for twenty-six years. He started business in 1850 and Thomas Glover and Sons was a grocery shop in the High Street until well into the twentieth century. Mr Glover's health was very good to the end and although ninety-one, he was still very active in the affairs of the town and church. His funeral the following Wednesday was conducted by the Revd L.H. Colls who had returned from St John's Wood specially for the service. The photograph shows the Revd Colls in the pulpit, while still a pastor. Directly below him is Mr Frederick Butcher, a well-known Tring banker and life-long friend of Mr Glover, who is sitting on his left, distinguished by his thick white beard.

When the war started on 4 August 1914 huts at Halton Camp were being prepared to house the soldiers but as they were not ready billets were hastily arranged in Tring. Frank Bly, then a ten-year-old boy, described how army officers, each with a policeman, divided the town into sections, visited every house, counted the rooms, counted the family and then came out and chalked on the wall K/4 and below it a number. It meant 'Kitchener's Fourth Army' and the number of men to be billeted there. By October the camp was ready and it was said that the soldiers had behaved so well that the Tring people were sorry to see them go.

As soon as the war started many of the young men volunteered for the army. As early as August four members of the Post Office staff joined their regiments, no doubt making it difficult to run the postal service. One of the first to volunteer was Tring born Eric Reed, his name being on a list of local men serving in the forces by November 1914. Born in King Street in 1884, Eric had trained as a blacksmith and farrier and so became a sergeant armourer with the King's Own Yorkshire Light Infantry. He served in Italy shoeing horses and mules and repairing carts and field guns. The mules were frequently used to bring wounded soldiers back from the battlefields in specially made panniers. Eric was fortunate enough to survive the war; sadly many young Tring men did not. He resumed his occupation of blacksmith, one of his jobs being to care for the feet of the zebras that the Hon. Walter Rothschild would use in harness.

In 1914 Lord Rothschild was having cottages built at Bunstrux Hill with the object of giving them to the council to house Tring families in need of a home. When the war started there were refugees coming from Belgium, desperately in need of homes. The council set up a War Refugees Committee and it was suggested that nine newly finished cottages should, with Lord Rothschild's permission, be made available to the refugees. In addition a group of people took over the house Woodville in Park Road, and by the end of October a family of eight were living there. They were Monsieur and Madame Rayée and their six children, who came from Ostend where they had a flourishing business until their country was overrun. The picture shows a group of Belgians at Aldbury.

In 1914 a group of farmers and friends met at the Rose and Crown Hotel and decided to form a new Sparrow Club. In 1891 there had been a Tring and District Sparrow Club and in 1892 a record number of 5,345 birds had been destroyed locally in five months, and 20,000 over the whole area. The farmers described the sparrows as 'impudent destructive little pests' and prizes were awarded to those members who killed the largest numbers. In 1914 the society offered to pay 3d a dozen for all sparrows' heads sent in by members. At the AGM in 1918 it was announced that 4,296 sparrows had been killed and £4 9s 6d had been paid in the past year. By 1922 the price per dozen heads had been increased to 6d so the 'total extermination' planned in the 1890s had obviously not gone according to plan. No records have been found of a Tring and District Sparrow Club since the 1920s.

The year 1915 saw the death of Lord Nathan ('Natty') Rothschild. Known as an immensely wealthy financier and, as his obituary describes, 'the arbiter of the destinies of nations', he was known and loved in Tring as a kind and considerate employer and generous benefactor to the townspeople. Born in the family mansion in Piccadilly on 8 November 1840, he died in March 1915 and was buried in the Jewish Cemetery, Willesden, on 2 April. A large party from Tring travelled to London to attend the funeral. He left a wife and two sons, Walter, who inherited the title, and Charles. His wife Emma Louisa, also his cousin, stayed in Tring and continued to take an interest in the town and its people. Her name lives on in the complex of homes specially adapted for some of Tring's older residents, known as Emma Rothschild Court.

Early in 1915 Tring heard that one of its young men, Edward Barber of the 1st Grenadier Guards, had been awarded the Victoria Cross for conspicuous bravery in France. Edward Barber was born at 40 King Street on 10 June 1893. He enlisted in the Guards in 1911 and was sent to France in 1914. He was the son of William and Sarah Ann Barber, later of Miswell Lane, and three other sons were also on active service. It was said at the time that

Tring people were not surprised that a Barber boy had won the VC, as they were a lively group of boys, always up to mischief. On hearing the sad news of his death a little later his parents said, 'He was afraid of nothing, no matter what it was. In all his boyish scrapes he was always plucky.' Mrs Barber, accompanied by her husband, received her son's VC from King George V at Buckingham Palace the following year. She survived to see another world war, dying at the age of eighty-two in 1943. Edward Barber's bravery was recorded in at least two series of cigarette cards depicting heroes of the armed forces.

Pte. EDWARD BARBER.

Cohen, Weenen & Co.'s
CIGARETTES

No. 87
PRIVATE
EDWARD BARBER
(1st Batt. Grenadier Guards)
At Neuve Chapelle, Barber ran in front of his grenade company, and bombed the enemy so effectively that many surrendered. When approached he was found quite unsupported with many still surrendering to him.
Photo: Farringdon

LONDON

Mr Cyril Howlett, pictured here on his wedding day, was another Tring man to serve in the war, as a driver in the Royal Flying Corps. His parents had the post office and general stores on the corner of Queen Street and King Street and he and his wife, Maud, whom he met in London during the war, took on the business after his father died. The premises known as Stratford House, were more recently the surgery of the popular doctor, Dr Plumm, and it is now a private house. Cyril is now perhaps best remembered as one of Tring's most capable photographers. Samples of his pictures feature in collections of early postcards. Starting photography while still in his teens, he sold postcard views of Tring in his parents' shop.

The cameras that Cyril Howlett used exist to this day. To a modern photographer they would seem cumbersome but they achieved very good results. The smaller one would have been used for field work and the larger one for studio photography, complete with a sturdy wooden tripod.

A wartime photograph of Mr Arthur Bagnall sitting in a very similar pose to that of 1911 when he was pictured with his young wife. He served with the Red Cross in France during the war as a sergeant and received a certificate in recognition of his services. Mr Bagnall was well known to most Tring people. As well as being a master tailor, having served apprenticeship under Mr Burch of New Mill, he was the deputy registrar from 1910 and the Tring agent for the Prudential Assurance Company. He was obviously a very busy man as he was also a Baptist lay preacher. He held services at the local villages, including Long Marston, Aldbury and Potten End. For many years he was superintendent of Wilstone Baptist Sunday School. He died on 30 November 1968 at the age of eighty-seven at his home, 1 Albert Street, where he had lived since his marriage fifty-eight years before.

This photograph shows Mr John Boarder of Gamnell, New Mill, with his little daughter, Lily. He had caught the large pike at Tring reservoirs on 27 December 1915. It was 3ft 6in long and weighed $16\frac{1}{2}$lbs. A retired policeman, John served as a food control inspector towards the end of the war and was a special constable in Tring until 1940 when he was seventy-three years old. He and his wife, Emily, celebrated their golden wedding on 25 January 1941 and their diamond wedding ten years later.

The best known statesman in the war was Field Marshal Lord Kitchener, Secretary of State for War, whose face on posters telling the young men of Britain that he needed them was seen all over the country. In March 1915 he paid a visit to Tring to inspect the troops who were being trained in the area. He appears to have been impressed with what he saw. Lord Kitchener was killed when HMS *Hampshire*, the ship on which he was travelling to Russia, hit a mine off the Orkneys in 1916. Genuine sorrow was felt in Tring, muffled peals were rung on the church bells and flags were flown at half-mast.

On the home front, an event took place at Tring post office to mark the retirement of Mr Henry Albert Reed after nearly forty years as a rural postman, walking daily to Cholesbury and back in the mornings and to Wilstone in the afternoons. The staff gathered to see Mr Reed presented with the Imperial Service medal, a bronze star with a silver centre. He also received an ornate certificate signed by the Postmaster General, Mr C. Hobhouse, for the faithful service he had rendered to the state during his working years. Born in 1855, Henry Reed became a postman after leaving school and on retirement became a gardener. He died in 1932. The photograph, obviously a carefully posed one, shows Mr Reed handing mail to someone on his round.

It would be impossible here to list all the young men of Tring who fought for their country in the First World War, many sadly not returning and now remembered on the Tring war memorial. Mr and Mrs Wells of Tring Ford received a letter from Buckingham Palace in September 1915, to say how much King George V appreciated the public spirit of their six sons who volunteered for services in His Majesty's Forces. This must have been an anxious time for the Wells family. Sadly one young man who did not return was Harry Prentice, son of Mr and Mrs F. Prentice of King Street. Although not quite seventeen he joined up at the beginning of the war and went to the front in May 1916 where he was killed two months later. Private Prentice, pictured here, belonged to the 2nd/1st Buckinghamshire Battalion, Oxfordshire and Buckinghamshire Light Infantry. Harry's younger brother, George, recalls that before his brother volunteered for the army at the age of sixteen he had been sent white feathers, a cruel practice branding the recipient a coward.

This beautiful plaque was issued to commemorate those men who had died in the war. This one is for Harry Prentice and it has been preserved by his family to this day. The original plaque is nearly five inches in diameter.

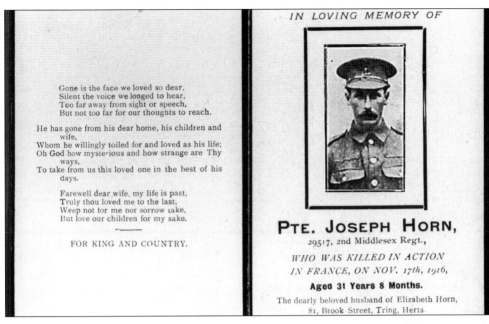

Gone is the face we loved so dear,
Silent the voice we longed to hear,
Too far away from sight or speech,
But not too far for our thoughts to reach.

He has gone from his dear home, his children and
   wife,
Whom he willingly toiled for and loved as his life;
Oh God how mysterious and how strange are Thy
   ways,
To take from us this loved one in the best of his
   days.

Farewell dear wife, my life is past,
Truly thou loved me to the last,
Weep not for me nor sorrow take,
But love our children for my sake.

FOR KING AND COUNTRY.

IN LOVING MEMORY OF

PTE. JOSEPH HORN,
29517, 2nd Middlesex Regt.,

*WHO WAS KILLED IN ACTION
IN FRANCE, ON NOV. 17th, 1916,*

Aged 31 Years 8 Months.

The dearly beloved husband of Elizabeth Horn,
81, Brook Street, Tring, Herts.

Many families in Tring received a card, like this one in memory of Private Joseph Horn, the husband of Mrs Elizabeth Horn of Brook Street, Tring. Born in Harrow Yard, Akeman Street, he was the son of James Horn and Emma Horn, née Delderfield. Joseph had only been in France since joining the army earlier in the year. The parish magazine when recording his death said, 'He died doing his duty and who could wish for a nobler death?' Doubtless this was of little consolation to his grieving family.

Another young Tring man tragically killed in France in 1916 was Herbert Hazzard of Chapel Street. He enlisted in the 1st Bucks Territorials in November 1914 and had been in France for the past year. Before joining the Army he had worked for Messrs Honour and Sons in Akeman Street as a machinist. In a letter to Pte Hazzard's parents his commander, Captain L.W. Crouch, described how fearless and cheerful their son always was and said 'I have lost one of my best men in your son and feel his loss most keenly.' One wonders how many letters like this were received by grieving wives and mothers in Tring. This portrait was taken shortly before Pte Hazzard went off in the Army.

In 1916 the Revd Claud T.T. Wood, only son of the Revd H.T. Wood, rector of Aldbury, was awarded the Military Cross for his services during military operations in the field. Early in the war he volunteered as a chaplain with the Herts Territorials. At that time he was serving as a curate to the Revd Lord William Cecil at Hatfield. In 1930 he came to Tring as the parish priest at St Peter and St Paul's church in the High Street. Later, in 1942, he left the town to take up an appointment as archdeacon at St Alban's Cathedral. In 1948, at the age of sixty-two, he was appointed the new Suffragan Bishop of Bedford and it was as Bishop Wood he gave his name to the junior mixed school in Frogmore Street, ensuring that he would be remembered forever by future generations of Tring children.

Sadly, the following year more Tring men were lost in the war, one of them being Driver Ralph Battson of the Royal Field Artillery, who died in hospital in France on 15 May 1917. As a member of the Tring Church Lads' Brigade, in those days run on rather military lines, Driver Battson volunteered for services in August 1914. He had been in France for nearly two years. In the First World War a lot of the transport was horse drawn and it was said that he was often complimented on the care he took of his horses. The parish magazine of June 1917 said: 'Even before the war broke out he was keen to be a soldier. When quite a small boy he joined our Church Lads' Brigade of which he was always a keen and smart member.'

Many of the young men at the beginning of the war, like Driver Battson, were eager to go to fight. A postcard, one of a large series, was issued at the time, marked 'Official War Photograph', showing hundreds of soldiers of the North Lancs Regiment cheering and waving their helmets in the air on being ordered to the trenches. The unfortunate horses did not volunteer. At the start of the war, Frank Bly, then ten years old, described how at the Tring Show in August officials from the army came and numbered and catalogued each horse, from farm horse to fine pedigree, ready to requisition them for service use. It is estimated that in the First World War around two million horses were killed. The photograph shows competitors at Tring Show in the class for mares and foals in happier times.

When this photograph was first seen it appeared that, being taken in the last year of the war, it showed local people packing ammunition into shell baskets. They are ex-howitzer shell baskets made for use during the war, but when a more efficient type was introduced Mr W.J. Rodwell of Tring Brewery purchased about 50,000 of the old ones. They were adapted to carry apples from Mr Rodwell's orchards on behalf of the Ministry of Food. This was described as a new industry brought on by the war and it employed nearly 100 people, mostly women, girls and boys. There were depots at the Old Malting, New Mill, the Royal Hotel, Tring station (pictured here), the Brewery, Tring and the Old Brewery, Wendover.

Another Tring man was decorated in 1918 when Sergeant Sidney Lovell of the 1st Bucks Battalion was awarded the Military Medal for gallantry in action. He was one of the first to join up and went out with his battalion in March 1915 for operations in France and Italy. He was wounded twice in action in France on the Somme and at Passchendaele, but made a good recovery and he was awarded the Military Medal in the campaign against the Austrian Army platoon. He was one of the fortunate ones and he returned to Tring where he married his wife, Florence, at the parish church on 21 April 1921. Living at 18 Longfield Road, they celebrated their golden wedding in 1971. Both Mr and Mrs Lovell were founder members of the Tring British Legion. This photograph taken before the First World War shows Sidney Lovell in the centre at the front and behind him on the left Edward Barber who became Tring's only recipient of the Victoria Cross.

On 27 November 1918 the unveiling of Tring's war memorial was performed by General Sir William Robertson DSO who was the General Officer in Chief, Great Britain. The Inns of Court OTC from Berkhamsted provided a guard of honour and a band. The photograph shows the Dean of Lincoln, on the left, with the vicar of Tring, the Revd Henry Francis, and General Robertson. The names of the men who had given their lives were not carved on the steps of the cross until the following year. The vicar said that they were anxious to know that the list was complete and accurate in every particular. This was especially important as the names were put on in alphabetical order. It was also proposed that a vellum book be kept in the church giving the names of the men, with their ranks, regiments and honours.

Tring was one of the first towns in the country to commission a war memorial to men lost in the war. The Early English cross was designed by P.M. Johnson FRIBA and many later memorials in other areas were based on Tring's design. Although finished before Armistice Day, it was wreathed in a large Union Jack to await the official unveiling on 27 November.

On 19 July 1919 the people of Tring gathered to celebrate the peace after the 1914-18 war. The Treaty of Versailles had been signed on 28 June. The soldiers who had returned asked that a short informal service should be conducted in front of the war memorial to honour those who had given their lives. The Revd Henry Francis conducted the service and two more in the church later in the day, to celebrate the National Day of Rejoicing. The names of 105 servicemen had been carved on the steps of the memorial. By 1924 Cllr Jabez Pratt complained of the poor condition of the war memorial, the letters having been painted several times. It was agreed that they should be leaded in and Mr Hobbs, the stonemason in Western Road, quoted £38 to lead in the 1,854 letters. The work commenced in July that year. This photograph is one of a series taken on the day from a window of the Rose and Crown. Most show the crowd from the back but here the service has obviously finished and the photographer has asked them to turn round.

Above: A sad, but perhaps not unexpected, event took place in October 1919: the death of Mr Frederick Butcher, at the age of ninety-three. He died at his home, Frogmore, off Frogmore Street where the Friars Walk estate now stands. The Butcher family had banks in Chesham, Aylesbury and Tring. The Tring branch is now the NatWest bank in the High Street. Mr Butcher, always a supporter of the Akeman Street Baptist church, was interred in the burial ground there, alongside his wife who had died in 1905. Again the Revd L.T. Colls came to Tring from St John's Wood to perform the ceremony. This photograph was taken outside houses in Park Street.

Opposite: Life was not entirely peaceful in Tring in 1919. There was the first of the so-called 'Great Strikes' aimed at bringing life to a standstill. Since a lot of local farmers and businessman relied on sending milk and produce to London it was a serious matter for Tring. To encourage lorry drivers to continue working, a local gentleman borrowed a pantechnicon from Messrs J. Gower and Sons and set up a free buffet on the church square for drivers and their mates. Hot coffee and cakes were served, which seemed to have helped the situation as it was reported that during the whole period there was an excellent supply of food for the district and traders were highly satisfied.

One of the best-loved ministers in Tring was the Revd Charles Pearce, pastor of the High Street Baptist church. He came from Thame in May 1851 as a draper, but devoted time to the Baptist church in Frogmore Street. Now a private house, it was once the Salvation Army headquarters. Mr Pearce decided to train for the ministry and once a pastor he worked tirelessly to raise funds to build the present High Street Baptist church. After nearly forty-six years, he tendered his resignation at the beginning of 1920, to take effect in March. As well as being a minister the Revd Pearce had also served as Chairman of the Urban District Council and earned the affection and respect of many Tring people. In May the same year he and his wife were presented with the sum of £792 0s 6d and an illuminated album containing the 646 signatures of those who had contributed to the gift.

After the war it was decided to give a 'Peace Souvenir' to the returned servicemen to express the town's appreciation of their part in gaining the eventual victory. An illuminated address was designed with a view of Tring from the Downs at the top. It was to be presented in an oak frame and signed by the joint chairmen, the Revd Charles Pearce of the High Street Free Baptist church and Frank J. Brown of Okeford, Christchurch Road, later Osmington School. It was not until 1920 that the certificates could be presented due to a post-war shortage of printing paper.

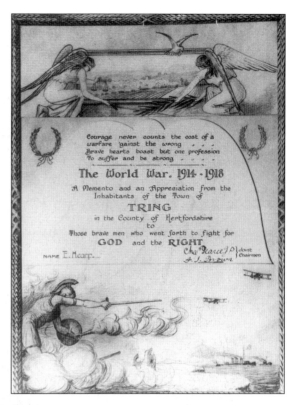

The recipient of this example was Mr Ernest Hearn, seen here with his wife and son. Earlier he had served as a private in the 1st Oxfordshire Light Infantry, being discharged from Lucknow in 1906 at the age of twenty-two. He was married soon after his return to civilian life. Early in 1915 he was one of eighty-six members of the Tring branch of the Ancient Order of Foresters to volunteer for the First World War and he rejoined his old regiment. During the action he was wounded but he was able to return to his wife and family at the end of the war. Like many Tring men he was known in the town by a nickname. His was 'Dixon'. The practice of calling men by nicknames was particularly prevalent in Wigginton where Tom Moy recorded that most Freds were known as 'Nipper' and most Arthurs as 'Happy'. An exception to this was a certain Arthur who was known as 'Grizzle'.

In the days when barges travelled the network of canals, carrying goods all over the country, an important Tring industry was Bushell Brothers' boat yard at New Mill. In 1920 they constructed the largest boat built this side of London for the London Haulage Company. It was 75ft long and had two engines providing 400hp. It was said to be capable of hauling six barges of 150 tons each at 5 knots. The completed boat weighed 100 tons and its size meant that on its way to be delivered to London there would be only one inch to spare when passing under the bridges. Fortunately when safely delivered to London the following year the large boat was destined to work on the Thames which provided a lot more room than the canals. The photograph of the canal and dockyard was taken at about this time.

In the back of the picture of the dockyard workers can be seen part of Mr W.N. Mead's flour mills, another source of employment for local people. Several generations of the Mead family lived in New Mill and were respected for their generous interest in the community, supporting, among other things, the church and various sports facilities. The mill, now called Heygates, is still a thriving business, providing local supermarkets with flour.

Three

1921-1930

Wigginton, like Tring, wanted to build a war memorial to honour the men of the village who gave their lives in the war. It was made in the form of a Celtic cross and the dedication ceremony was performed on Sunday 3 January 1921. A procession was led by local ex-servicemen, followed by a cross bearer, the choir and the clergy. The Bishop of Lichfield gave an address before Lord Kitchener of Khartoum stood on the steps to unveil the memorial. This was the son of the Lord Kitchener who lost his life in 1916. At the end of the ceremony the bishop said a prayer of dedication and read the names of the twenty-three men who appeared on the memorial.

This carefully posed photograph shows the wedding of Lizzie Drake of Drayton Beauchamp and Syd Baldwin of New Mill which took place on 26 April 1921 at four o'clock, at St Mary's church, Drayton Beauchamp. Mr Baldwin's brother, Walter, was best man and the bridesmaids were Nora Drake, the bride's sister, and May Saunders, the groom's niece. The Baldwin family had a butchers shop at 21 Gamnell, New Mill, and the wedding was held late in the day as the brothers were occupied in the shop until after mid-afternoon. They then went to the wedding in a pony and trap. The reception was held at the Church Hall at Drayton Beauchamp and later the happy couple made their home over the family butchers shop in New Mill.

The summer of 1921 was an exceptionally hot one, prompting Messrs Rodwell of Akeman Street to comment on the unprecedented demand for their mineral waters. Young people cooled off by swimming in the reservoirs. For an inexperienced swimmer this was not always wise as the water was deep and the weeds were treacherous. In July of 1921 George Nash of King Street got into difficulties through becoming entangled in weeds and was in danger of drowning. Ernest Wright of Chapel Street, just getting dressed on the bank, jumped in and managed to pull him to safety and after artificial respiration was applied for a while George recovered. In October the Royal Humane Society awarded a vellum certificate to Ernest and it was presented at a special meeting of Tring Council. This photograph shows cubs of the Tring 1st Scout Group in the early 1930s. One seldom sees swimmers in the reservoirs these days.

In 1921 the third Earl Brownlow of the Ashridge Estate died. The fourth earl, who already had a home, Belton Court, found that, faced with heavy death duties, he could not keep up both properties and the trustees were instructed to sell the house and over 3,000 acres of parkland. Local people were horrified that the estate would be broken up and their efforts led to the eventual acquisition of most of the Ashridge parklands by the National Trust. The house, and some surrounding acres, were brought by Urban Broughton and became a residential college. During the Second World War the house was used as a hospital, catering for soldiers and civilians mainly from London. After the war it resumed its peacetime role, now known as Ashridge Management College.

Ashridge Monument.

Ashridge is still popular with visitors. Walkers can see magnificent old trees and an abundance of bluebells, foxgloves and rhododendrons. The gardens round the house, even before the estate was sold, would be open to the public in aid of charity. Recently the National Trust have improved their restaurant facilities near the Bridgewater monument, pictured here, and made a lot of the paths more accessible to wheelchair users. The monument was put up in memory of the third Duke of Bridgewater who masterminded the building of the local canal network in the eighteenth century. These canals were important to the trade and prosperity of Tring and still provide leisure facilities for walkers and boat enthusiasts.

The war memorials of Marsworth and Long Marston were unveiled by Lord Rothschild on the same day, Sunday 7 August 1921. The Marsworth memorial in the form of a Gothic cross was erected in the churchyard. Mr A.J. Gurney, a Marsworth architect, did not charge for the design, and Mr W.N. Mead of Tring purchased the Portland stone that was used in the construction. The cost of the finished memorial, about £140, was raised by public subscription. Fifty-five men of Marsworth served in the Great War. The names of eleven who did not return were inscribed on the base of the cross. Lord Rothschild made a speech before unveiling the memorial. The Last Post was sounded by members of the Wendover Boys' Brigade and their band led the singing of the National Anthem and a hymn before wreaths were placed at the base by relatives of the fallen. Lord Rothschild then went on to Long Marston.

The Long Marston memorial was a Celtic cross carved out of a single slab of silver grey granite on three wide steps of the same stone. It was erected in the main road of the village near the school buildings. After the proposed turf surround with a neat rail fence and ornamental trees were added it was estimated that the total cost would be about £400. The names of the ten Long Marston men who lost their lives were inscribed on the memorial. The Long Marston Band played music as people assembled for the ceremony and ex-servicemen formed a guard of honour. The 39th West London Troop of Boy Scouts were camping in the vicinity and two of their officers acted as standard bearers. The vicar of Long Marston, the Rev. H.M. Rowden, held a short service before Lord Rothschild made a speech and removed the Union Jack covering the cross. Again relatives and friends laid their floral tributes on the steps. On the right of this photograph can be seen the village school that was demolished by a bomb in the next war.

A little later in 1921, on Sunday 3 October, the Wilstone war memorial, a Celtic cross, was unveiled by Captain G.M. Brown MC of Tring. The cross was made of granite and was set on a base of stone that earlier had formed a part of the swing bridge over the Wendover Arm of the Grand Junction Canal. Railings round the memorial were given by Mr P. Mead and nine names were carved on the base. The cost was approximately £140. The unveiling ceremony was conducted by the Revd H.M. Rowden, vicar of Long Marston, with the Long Marston Band playing the music for the hymns. The vicar was aided by the Revd F.G. Kemp, Baptist minister of New Mill. Mr Mead read the names of the fallen and then Captain Brown removed the flag from the cross and spoke to the crowd. After a minutes silence a prayer was said by Mr Arthur Bagnall of Tring, representing Wilstone Baptist church, and the band played the Last Post. This was followed by the Reveille sounded by RAF trumpeters, and wreaths were placed on the memorial.

Towards the end of 1921 there was an auction held at the Rose and Crown Hotel by Messrs Brown and Co. For sale was the Tring post office, at that time let to the Postmaster General at £120 per annum. The auctioneer suggested several other uses to which the property could be adapted and several bidders were interested but it was finally purchased by the Postmaster General for £1,850. This building housed Tring's main post office for many years. When this was closed the post office business moved further down the High Street to a shop that in earlier days had been Glovers the grocers. The large building for some time was used as a bathroom company's showroom and is now an Italian restaurant

After the war many ex-servicemen belonged to a society with the rather cumbersome title of The Tring and District Branch of the National Federation of Demobilised and Discharged Soldiers. In 1921 this was absorbed into the British Legion and played an important part in the life of the town. As well as a clubroom in the Church House, open every evening for members, the Legion's events each year included their popular fête on August Bank Holiday Monday and a procession to the war memorial on Remembrance Sunday in November. Processions to the park were often led by the British Legion Band, seen here having just turned into Akeman Street, past Alex Smith's chemists shop on the corner. In the background the white building is Mr Stevens' cycle shop advertising 'Yusemee' cycles.

In the autumn of 1921 painters were employed to redecorate the new Market House. When cleaning the old bell that hung over the building they found traces of lettering on it. After considerable effort to clean away the dirt the inscription was found to read 'Henry Guy, Esquier, Tring Park in the County of Hertfordshire 1680'. Mr Guy was one of the early owners of Tring Park and the date records the time that King Charles II granted Henry Guy, and succeeding owners, a charter giving him the right to hold a market in Tring and to receive the tolls from it. When the new Market House was built in 1900 Lord Rothschild forfeited his market rights and transferred them to Tring Council on behalf of the town. The bell, with its quaint old-fashioned spelling of the word 'esquire', no longer hangs over the Market House but is housed inside the council chambers.

In June 1922 Mr Frank Charles Clement of the Tring family of jewellers and watchmakers had a successful day at the RAC 3-litre Tourist Trophy on the Isle of Man. He came second in a four cylinder Bentley and completed eight circuits of the 38-mile course in just under 5 hours 29 minutes. Mr Clement was invited in 1920 to take part in experimental work for Bentley and to race their cars. In 1921 he drove the first Bentley to victory at Brooklands. From 1923 to 1930 he drove in every 24-hour Le Mans race and was placed in all of them. In 1929, with co-driver Jack Barclay, he won the 500-mile race at Brooklands in a 4.3 litre Bentley at an average of over 107mph. Mr Clement died in 1970 at the age of eighty-three.

Miss Katherine Mary Wright, pictured here, was the youngest of the eight daughters of Mr and Mrs A.E. Wright and the last one to get married. She married Mr H. Venables at St Clement's church, Fulham, on Saturday 10 June 1923. She was well known in Tring, having been on the staff of Tring post office. The best man was Albert Venables and the bridesmaids were Doreen Howlett, Dorothy Bagnell, Ivy Sargent, May and Bertha Durrant and Ivy Kimber.

Joseph Grout Williams, Tring's largest landowner after Lord Rothschild, died at Pendley Manor on 9 October 1923 aged seventy-five. When Mr Williams inherited the Pendley estate in 1871 there was no house and he rented Tring Park until the lease ran out and Lord Rothschild bought the estate. While a new Pendley Manor was being built he rented Chequers, now the country residence of the Prime Minister. The shire horses of the Pendley stud were chosen to carry the coffin to Aldbury church where the funeral service was conducted on 13 October by the Rector of Aldbury, Canon Wood, assisted by the Revd Claud Wood from Croydon, the Revd T.V. Garnier from Tring and the Revd H.C. Finch from Wigginton. Mr Williams had been churchwarden at Tring for over forty years and while the funeral service was being conducted at Aldbury a memorial service was held in Tring by the Revd S. Mead. The photograph shows the coffin about to leave Pendley Manor.

On 26 July 1924, seventy-two cottages were put up for sale by the trustees of the Tring Park Estate. They were in Tring, Wilstone, Marsworth, Wigginton, Hastoe and Buckland Common. In Tring Lots 1, 2 and 3 were the three blocks of semi-detached houses near the bottom of Miswell Lane. They were described as being a pair of modern dwelling houses, exceptionally well built of brick with a tiled roof and in excellent repair throughout. They had mains water from the Chiltern Hills Spring Water Company and mains drainage. Each had three bedrooms and a good-sized garden. The six houses all had tenants, each paying 2s 6d per week. They were built in 1901. Lot 1 had Mr W. Stevens and Mr H. Hinton as tenants and was bought by Mr Kempster for £620. Lot 2 with tenants Mr J. Gascoine and Mr H. Burch was sold for £600 and Lot 3, with Mr J. Hedges and Mr T. Foster, was bought by Mr Bly for £600. The houses in this row have been extended over the years but still look much as they did here in 1924.

In March 1924 Tring lost one of its oldest inhabitants, James Griffin of Eastcroft, in his ninety-second year. He was born at Folly Farm, Long Marston but as a young man he spent some time in the post office service in Melbourne, Australia. He returned to England to take over the farm when his father died. He was remembered in Aylesbury as he was the generous donor of the John Hampden statue in the Market Square. John Hampden, of Hampden in Buckinghamshire, fought on the Parliamentary side in the Civil War and died of his wounds in 1643. The statue is said to depict him pointing to his birthplace. Another generous gesture by Mr Griffin was his support of the Royal Bucks Hospital in Aylesbury. Each year he donated £1 for every year of his age, his last contribution being £91. He also helped many causes closer to home and several of the stained-glass windows in Drayton Beauchamp church were donated by him. His funeral was held there on the afternoon of Thursday 7 March 1924.

In 1925 David Cornwall of Tring Park Cricket Club's Second XI had a remarkable success as a bowler. He took 56 wickets during the season but the event that hit the headlines was when he took all ten wickets in a match against Boxmoor. For this fine bowling performance he was given the ball used in the match, suitably inscribed as a memento of the day. He was also presented with a beautifully bound album containing photographs of 'Famous Cricketers' which had been presented to the committee by the retiring treasurer, William Smith. Mr Smith had held the post for thirty-eight years. David thanked the committee for the gifts and praised George Dinnage for his help as wicketkeeper. From left to right, back row: Fred Howlett, Sgt T. Lennard, Charles Rodwell (captain), Fred Cox. Middle row: David Cornwall, George Dinnage, Jim Budd, Frank Rogers. Front row: Horace Bandy, S. Dawe, Edward Bell.

Lady Rothschild was a generous benefactor to the town and provided a nurse to assist the local people. A lady named Nurse Giradet came in the first decade of the century and in 1916 it was announced that she had been awarded the newly introduced Royal Red Cross suggesting that as it was wartime she had used her nursing skills for the benefit of injured serviceman. Later the local nurse was Nurse Shore, still remembered by older Tring people. She founded a Infant Welfare Centre in Tring and in 1925 over a hundred mothers who attended the centre expressed their appreciation by presenting her with an attaché case, perhaps a suitable gift for a nurse who might have to dash off to help a Tring baby into the world at a moment's notice. Nurse Shore organised baby shows at local events, arranging for doctors to come as judges. At a fête at Pendley Manor in June 1934 the winner of the class for babies aged one or two years was baby Phyllis Killick, who can be seen as a six-year-old in 1939 on page 130, still tiny compared with the large horse she is feeding. In the group photograph Nurse Shore is in the centre of the front row at a baby show she had organised in the early thirties for the Tring British Legion. The babies here would now all be pensioners.

This photograph of Nurse Shore with the Red Cross nurses was taken early in the Second World War when she assisted at the Tring Minor Ailments Clinic. The Red Cross nurses trained in the old stable block at the mansion. The doctor on the left of the picture is unknown. The three nurses are Barbara Jones and Mrs Marshall at the back and Dorothy Keen in the front of them.

In 1924 the Champneys Estate at Wigginton was put up for sale by Messrs W. Brown and Co. of Tring. There are records of a house at Champneys as far back as the beginning of the fourteenth century and there was a succession of owners until it was purchased in 1902 by Nathaniel Rothschild of Tring Park as a dower house for his wife, Emma, should she wish to leave Tring in later life. She did not and over twenty years later, some time after the death of her husband, she sold the estate for the sum of £27,000. By 1925 Champneys had been acquired by the osteopath, Stanley Lief, and he opened his well-known Nature Cure Resort. It has changed hands over the years and is popular to this day for people who want to escape for a while from busy lives and to be pampered in comfortable surroundings. This photograph shows Champneys after Mr Lief had added to both sides of the main building.

Mr J.G. Williams of Pendley Manor was a churchwarden of Tring parish church for forty years. To commemorate his life Mrs Williams commissioned a stained-glass window to be placed in the North transept of the church. It was unveiled by Mr William's nephew, Major Vivian Williams of Towcester, at Choral Evensong on Easter Eve 1926. The vicar, the Revd T.V. Garnier, took the service and many members of the Williams family were present. The subject of the window is the Epiphany and in the three top panels are depicted St Andrew, St Augustine and St Anselm. Visitors to Tring can still admire this beautiful stained-glass window when visiting the church.

Another stained-glass window was commissioned for Tring parish church in 1926, this time to be put in the wall of the Lady Chapel on the south side. It was to commemorate the late Revd Henry Francis, sometime vicar of Tring and afterwards the Dean of Battle near Hastings. Mr J. Hobbs, who had his stonemasons yard in Western Road, completed the masonry work for the window and the dedication ceremony was performed at Evensong on Friday 30 July by the Archdeacon of St Albans, the Ven. and Hon. Kenneth Gibbs. Thus in one year Tring church gained two beautiful new stained-glass windows.

This photograph taken at Christmas 1926 shows Mr Baldwin's butchers shop at New Mill, with their display of beef, lamb and pork. Although these days meat would never be hung outside, with all the insistence on hygiene, the animals then would have been bred locally and killed on the butcher's premises. The meat came from Mr Reuben Bedford's New Ground Farm. Mr Bedford also owned the shop but it was known to local people as 'Baldwins Butchers' as Sid Baldwin was the manager there for thirty-nine years. Some of the Christmas supplies would have come from Smithfield market to meet the increased demand. More recently the butchers, now closed, was Gregory's. In front of the shop decorated for Christmas are, from left to right, Harry Pargeter, Sid Baldwin, Stanley Randall and Ted Goodgame.

In 1927 a new vicarage was built. The old vicarage behind the church, now occupied by the Sutton Housing Trust, was the home of Tring vicars until 1920. Many complained of the expense of keeping the building going and the Revd T.V. Garnier spoke about the problems of living in a large house too big for one's income and with too large a garden. In 1920 he let the vicarage to Mr M.C. Kemp, the well-known Harrow master and famous cricketer, and he moved to a smaller house. This early photograph of the old vicarage was taken from the church tower.

When the new vicarage, seen here, was built in 1927 it surprised local people who saw it as another large building. The Revd Garnier defended it as much more economical, it having only one bathroom, five bedrooms and a study, in addition to the usual living rooms. The garden does appear to still require quite a bit of keeping up. The new vicarage was built on land at the bottom of Mortimer Hill and later in the century it was demolished to make way for the houses that are now Mortimer Rise.

The Tring fire brigade's engine was pulled by a team of horses until the 1920s. As late as 1926 they were still using the old engine, pulling it with a lorry if horses were not available. There had been criticism on several occasions of the slow response to a call to a fire and the council's first suggestion in 1926 was to hire a motor fire engine to test its efficiency. Early in 1927, after the fire brigade committee had witnessed a demonstration of a modern fire engine at Woodbridge, it was decided to purchase one for Tring and the surrounding villages. Wigginton Parish Council was concerned that the new engine would not manage to climb the steep hill up to their village. In early days more horses would have been added to the team. In June 1927 it was decided to take out a loan of £600 to purchase the new fire engine and if the neighbouring parishes would contribute, it would only add a penny to the rates. The new Baico-Tonna motor fire engine arrived in October and tests done in November proved that it was capable of climbing the hills, through rather slowly when carrying the full team of firemen. It had not been uncommon for all the firemen to climb down from the engine and walk up the hill to spare the horses. This early photograph shows Tring fire brigade outside the Mansion Gates in the 1920s. From left to right, back row: Mr Reeves, Will Cooper, Ernie Roberts, William Keele, Sid Lovell, Edward Brittain. Front row: Harry Bull, George Hinton, William (Duke) Welling, George Putnam, Eddie Brackley, Fred Rance, Peter Farr.

The YMCA and the YWCA had a large membership in Tring. Here in this posed photograph by George Bell the boys and girls are pictured before a gymnastic display in the Victoria Hall. In the spring of 1927 the team gave a display there followed by a one-act temperance drama entitled 'Business as usual during the alterations'. The YMCA exhibitions were often given to raise money for local charities.

This photograph shows the YMCA team posing on the space opposite the Victoria Hall in Akeman Street, now a car park. This group of gymnasts includes Sid Horn, Frank Bly, Jack Lines and on the right the trainer, Sid Lovell.

In April 1927 Mr Vaisey, clerk to the council, felt that it was time for him to retire. In appreciation of his devoted service the council members gave him an illuminated address and commissioned a studio portrait of him to be taken. They requested that Mr Vaisey would allow them to keep the portrait in the Council Chamber were it still hangs. Affixed to the frame was a plate with the words: 'Arthur William Vaisey, clerk to the Tring Local Board 1877 to 1895 and to Tring Urban District Council 1895 to 1927. This portrait was presented on Mr Vaisey's retirement by the past and present members of the Tring Urban District Council in appreciation of his public service for a period of fifty years.' Looking at this photograph one feels that Mr Vaisey was a kindly, capable man.

The Tring Amateur Operatic and Dramatic Society had one of their greatest successes in February 1928 when they performed *The Rebel Maid* on five successive evenings at the Victoria Hall. It tells the story of the revolution of 1688 when William of Orange landed in England and became William III, and was described as 'refreshingly and typically English'. This shows Mr Frank Rogers as Solomon Hooker, the hero's servant. His performance was mentioned in the review of the opera. The 'serving maids' include, on his left, Mabel Warrior, later Mrs Goodliffe, as a member of the chorus.

This photograph shows a gun carriage with the coffin of Private James Osborne VC who had died in February 1928 at the age of seventy. Although Private Osborne had served with the 58th Northamptonshire Regiment his funeral was at Wigginton as he was born there and lived there for so many years, where he was known as 'Jacko'. He won his VC for conspicuous bravery at the assault on the Inhlobane mountain in Zululand on 2 February 1881. Although under fire from over forty Boers he picked up a wounded comrade, Private Mayes, put him across his horse and galloped back to camp. Many years later he attended a garden party given for the holders of the Victoria Cross by King George V. The funeral was conducted with full military honours. An RAF detachment from Halton formed the firing party and a group from the Northamptonshire Regiment also attended, their buglers, seen here, sounded the Last Post. The Rev. Tyrwhitt Drake conducted the service at Wigginton parish church.

This portrait shows 'Jacko' Osborne in uniform wearing his medal. *The Times of Natal*, published on Monday 1 May 1882, reported on the presentation of Private Osborne's VC and gave a description of the brave deed that deserved it. It would appear that he was fortunate to get back safely as a Boer bullet struck the stock of his rifle. Private Mayes was wounded in the leg but after the doctor removed the bullet he made a good recovery. At the presentation Lt-Gen. Smythe made a speech and read a letter from the War Office stating that HM Queen Victoria was pleased to confer the VC on Pte James Osborne.

Mr J.G. Williams of Pendley Manor, who died in 1923, was a churchwarden of Tring parish church for forty years. In his memory his wife donated a stained-glass window and in 1928 a new altar and reredos, designed by Mr W.E. Howard, were commissioned by her. They were dedicated by the Bishop of St Albans in June of that year. This early photograph, showing the previous reredos with its beautiful carved woodwork, would suggest its removal seemed hardly necessary, but later there were reports of an infestation of deathwatch beetle on the interior woodwork of the building so perhaps the old reredos had also been attacked. The area has now been cleared, giving a better view of the altar and the east end of the church.

For Mr and Mrs Tom Nutkins of 17 Park Road 1928 was a very special year as they celebrated their golden wedding anniversary. They were married at Tring church on 18 September 1878 by the curate, the Revd W. Walford. Mr Nutkins was employed on the Tring Park Estate for fifty years and had retired just two years before, at the age of seventy. They celebrated the day with three daughters, their sons-in-law and six grandchildren. Ten years later, on celebrating their diamond wedding, they received a telegram of congratulations from the King and Queen. Here Mr and Mrs Nutkins stand outside their home with their three daughters, Agnes, later Mrs Bushell; Nance, later Mrs Hummerston; and Eleanor, who became Mrs Fulks.

In 1928 it was announced that several acres of woodland at Whipsnade, between Tring and Dunstable, were being prepared as a 'country estate' for zoo animals. Although London Zoo was a popular tourist attraction some people had been worried about the cramped conditions and boredom of some animals. Clearings were made and some animals were introduced once the stout perimeter fence was completed, as this early photograph of the bison shows. The zoo was expected to be completed in two or three years' time, and today, known as Whipsnade Wild Animal Park, it still attracts a large number of visitors.

The large landmark of a huge white lion cut in the hillside can be seen for miles. During the Second World War it was 'camouflaged' for the duration, but restored afterwards. Whipsnade provides a wonderful day out, especially for children, and it has been popularised by television programmes in recent years.

Between the wars most people grew their own vegetables in their gardens and plots of land were taken over for allotments. Those between Duckmore Lane and the Aylesbury Road were purchased from Lord Rothschild in 1920 and many are still cultivated today. An Allotment Holders' Association was founded in 1924 and at their annual show prizes would given for the best produce. In New Mill Mr N.W. Mead gave a cup for the best-kept allotment. It was won in 1930 by Mr Jack Drake, who won it for three years and was therefore allowed to keep it. Mr Mead gave another cup and Mr Drake won it for another two years. His success was undoubtedly due in part to the help given to him by his two sons, George and Bill, seen here on each side of Mr Mead who is presenting the cup to their father.

When the old Market House opposite the Rose and Crown was knocked down in 1900 it left an open area known as The Square. Soon, however, with the coming of the motor car, it was frequently used as a car park. Councillor Miss Boyson was concerned about this and in 1930 raised the subject with the council. She felt that the area in front of the war memorial should not be filled with cars and buses. Another concern was that the cellars beneath the old Market House were said to have been filled with laths and plaster from the demolition and it was debatable whether the area was safe for buses. It remained a parking area for many more years and it was much later that cars were banned and the 'zebra maze' added as a reminder of Lord Rothschild and his trained zebras.

The Marsworth Operatic Guild's *Princess Ju Ju*, presented at the Parish Hall for three days in April 1930, seems to have been based rather loosely on Gilbert and Sullivan's *The Mikado*. There was a Lord Very High Executioner played with relish by Mr J. Reeve. There were guards, Lip Lip and Aye Aye played by J. Gates and S. Gregory. In the title role was Miss M. Miller and the Emperor Hokipokitippitoptop was Mr Edward Bell. Other parts were taken by Messrs W. Christopher, S. Pearson, T. Pratt, F. Reeve, R. Plumridge and T. Sear and the Misses E. Pratt, G. Cowdery, A. Gates, H. Scratcher, B. Gates, A. Reeve, A. Jellis, B. Hutchinson, E. Curtis and V. Andrews. The proceeds from the three well attended performances went to the All Saints Guild Fund.

Nearby Berkhamsted Castle, where William the Conqueror was said to been offered the crown of England by the Archbishop of York, Bishop Aldred, in 1066, was advertised in the Tring papers as 'a place to spend a happy day'. The castle was, of course, in ruins but the castle grounds made a pleasant venue for local events. In 1930 the Office of Works decided to repair the area where necessary and restore the moats as far as possible. This gave employment to 170 men, most of them from poor areas, and it was hoped the work would be completed by April 1931. This photograph shows a pageant there in June 1931.

Four

1931-1940

The Tring Amateur Operatic and Dramatic Society was formed early in 1922. For many years they concentrated on the operatic side, specialising in the musical comedies of Gilbert and Sullivan. In early 1931 they chose what was described as a dramatic work, *The Whole Town's Talking*. It was obviously more of a comedy as it told the story of an eligible young lady alternating between two rivals. This photograph, taken by Tring photographer Mr George Bell, shows the cast on the stage of the Victoria Hall. They include Frank Rogers, Doris Rogers, Mrs Woodward, Frederick Keen, Arthur Messenger, Beatrice Hobson, Dorothy Keen, Dorothy Cumming, Molly Tew, Charles Lee, V. Coldwell, L. Perkins, C. Peak, and Roland Rance. The furniture for the performance was lent by Mr John Bly.

Tring was a farming community and it was accepted that the more wealthy farmers and landowners would hunt with hounds. A more acceptable form of hunting to a lot of people today would have been that of the Tring Farmers Draghounds, where hounds followed a carefully laid trail across the local countryside. In 1931 Mr Herbert Grange, who had been a master for many years, celebrated his seventieth birthday. At a meet from his home, Tring Grove, on 14 February a birthday hunting party was held and light refreshments and birthday cake were supplied before the hounds moved off. The photograph of the meet shows Mr Herbert Grange in the foreground on the right.

The little girl in the this photograph is nine-year-old Ann Phipps, the daughter of Captain Phipps, the huntsman of the draghounds, and its youngest member, congratulating Mr Grange on attaining his seventieth birthday. It was said that Mr Grange's expertise over the jumps was the envy of many of the younger riders.

In 1931 a new cricket pavilion was opened in New Mill, thanks to the generosity of Mr William N. Mead of Tring Flour Mills. At the opening ceremony young Vera Welling is presenting a bouquet to Mrs Wood, wife of the Revd Claude Wood, later the Bishop of Bedford. On the left is Mr Arthur Vaisey. On the right stands Mr Arthur Underwood who had an undertakers business in New Mill from 1922 to 1936 and beside him is Mr Freeman.

In 1931 a major change took place in Tring schools, when it was decided to have mixed classes of boys and girls. Miss Stoner, headmistress of the Girls' Junior School, retired and Miss Winifred Baker came from St Mary's Mixed School in Hitchin, to be head of Tring's Junior Mixed School. It was a post she held for many years, and memories of her from her ex-pupils are varied and interesting. She retired at the end of the Easter term in 1967 after more than thirty-five years.

Several members of the Wright family were connected with the garage and coachbuilders in Western Road. The bride's father, R. George Wright, joined his cousin A.S. Wright in 1911, when George Parrott decided to retire. Mr Parrott was the founder and took A.S. Wright into partnership in 1902. Thus in 1911 it became Wright and Wright and the garage remained in the Wright family until 1969. The bride is Agnes Muriel Wright, twin daughter of Mr and Mrs R.G. Wright, and the bridegroom Joseph William Noel Orton from Birmingham. The wedding was at the Akeman Street Baptist church on Wednesday 12 August and Pastor S.E. Gerrard officiated. The bridesmaids were Marjorie and Constance Wright, the bride's sisters, Agnes Orton, the groom's sister, and Nina Simmons. Miss Simmons was to be a bride herself two years later when she married Frank Bly.

This photograph shows three members of a remarkably long-lived family. Mr John Wright, seen here on the right, was ninety-one in October 1932. His brother, Jesse, in the centre was ninety-two the previous January and his other brother, Albert, on the left was seventy-eight. They also had a sister, aged eighty-five, making a total for the four of 346 years! The brothers were connected with the butchers business in Akeman Street, Wright and Sons, founded by their father, George Wright, and all had lived in Tring all their lives. Sadly the September of the following year saw the death of two of the brothers, Albert and Jesse, within days of each other.

The Junior Imperial League was an intensely patriotic society for young people with ideals that seem rather out of date these days, when Britain no longer has an empire spread over half the world. Here the Junior Imps are enjoying a New Year Party on Wednesday evening, 6 February 1932 at the Junior YMCA Rooms, Akeman Street. The idea was to dress suitably for a 'Tramps' Supper', to bring food wrapped in gaily coloured handkerchiefs and to have a pennyworth of tea or coffee from 'Ye Olde Thirsty Sole' coffee stall, all supposedly 'outdoors'. The costumes were judged and the winners were Mabel Warrior and Stan Minall. In the photograph are, from left to right, back row: George Bell, Stan Minall, Doug Westcott, D. Campbell, R. Springham, R. Pearce, George Goodliffe (seated), W.O.H. Taylor, Minna Blount, C. Rodwell, Mabel Warrior, P. Newman, F. Mead, S. Brown, D. Dunkin, Cissie Bly, E. Childs. Front row: I. Desborough, S. Burton, C. Lester, A. Coningsby, R. Hughes, Edna Cowen, Kathleen Westcott, K. Collins.

The Tring British Legion was started in 1921.There was an enthusiastic membership and for a nominal fee of 5s a year they had full use of the clubroom, then at the Church House in Western Road. It opened from 7.30 to 10.30 every evening. The British Legion organised the events of Remembrance Day each November and in 1932 they held the first of the many August Bank Holiday Fêtes in Tring Park. This photograph shows the opening ceremony performed from the bandstand by Vice Admiral Silver CBE supported by a group of well-known Tring people including the vicar, the Revd C.T.T. Wood.

The fête would include sports events, a carnival, stalls and side-shows, fancy dress classes and a baby show organised by Nurse Shore. This photograph shows the class for decorated prams and it was won by 'Miss England III' put together by Mrs Sidney Lovell with her baby son in the driving seat. It is one of a set of photographs taken at the 1932 fête. It was clear that the people of Tring were prepared to wholeheartedly support the British Legion's enterprise as 1,500 admission tickets were sold before the event and nearly a 1,000 on the day.

On Wednesday 22 March 1933 the members of the Tring fire brigade met at the Bell Hotel to present Fireman Frederick James Reeve with this handsome chiming clock to mark his retirement after forty years. Born in Tring in 1873, Mr Reeve started with the brigade as a 'caller-up' when there was a fire, blowing a whistle to call out the volunteers. In 1910 he became a fireman under Captain Gilbert Grace. The presentation was made by Chief Officer George Putnam, who went on to be captain for many years. Mr Reeve was an enthusiastic bell-ringer for most of his life and was captain of the bell-ringers at Tring parish church. He also travelled all over England visiting other churches to join their teams of bell-ringers and try out different bells. This photograph shows Mr Reeve in his off-duty uniform. In the case of a fire he would have worn a large brass helmet as seen in the photograph below.

On Whit Monday 1933 the National Fire Brigade Association (South Midlands District) at West Drayton, Middlesex, held a district drill meeting with members of the fire brigades from all over the district competing. The Tring team had a successful day, winning the Winifred Graham Cup for the drill and the second prize for the hose cart second division drill. The team, pictured here with their certificate and trophies, comprised: Driver William Keele, Firemen P. Farr, Sid Lovell (trainer), E. Roberts and Harry Bull.

A wedding on Wednesday 8 February 1933 was not in Tring but was of considerable interest to the people of the town. At the church of the Holy Trinity, Old Wolverton, the bridegroom was Frank John Bly, only son of John Bly, the chairman of the District Council, and Mrs Bly of the antique shop in the High Street. His bride was Nina Kathleen Simmons of Stony Stratford. She had been a member of staff at Tring post office. Mr Bly was a prominent member of Tring YMCA and a member of the gymnast team. The best man was H.S. Wright, a cousin of the bridegroom, and the bridesmaids were Aileen Wilmin, Nellie and Phyllis Wright and Daphne Sharp. Frank Bly took over the antiques business from his father and was succeeded by his son, the present John Bly.

In 1934 work started on the new Scout hut in Longfield Road. The site had been given by Mrs Stenhouse of Harvieston, whose son, Norman Stenhouse, was Scoutmaster of the 1st Tring Troop. Most of the work was done by the Rovers and Scouts themselves. The new hut, which measured 50ft by 20ft, was divided into a large Scouts' room, a Cubs' room and a Rover Den. The cost had been £150 8s 7½ d. The Scout hut still stands in Longfield Road. Here, Mr Stenhouse is studying the plans.

Here are the successful New Mill tug-of-war team in 1934 when they won the Wigginton Fayre Challenge Cup. Many teams were connected with local pubs, this one came from the Queens Arms at New Mill, run by Fred Philby. He also had a business hiring out farm machinery and the team used to train by pulling one of his threshing engines across the fields. The team comprises, from left to right, back row: Tommy Welling, George Drake, Bill Richards, George Turner, Fred Philby. Front row: Jimmy Hills, 'Dine' Harding, Sid Baldwin, Bill Drake, 'Sonny' Keen.

On 19 November 1935 the Scout hut was formally opened by Sir Percy Everett, the County Boy Scout Commissioner for Hertfordshire. He made a speech on what he described as a 'foul night' and was pleased to find that so many Scouts and their parents had turned out for the occasion. He praised the efforts that had been made to build the new hut and, while not saying that every Scout was perfect, said they had 'dirty knees but clean minds'. He then handed over the deeds to Scoutmaster Stenhouse for safekeeping. The photograph shows, left to right, Aldbury Group Scoutmaster, Norman Shaw, G. Kenyon-Bell, Sir Percy Everett, Norman Stenhouse, Mrs Stenhouse who gave the site, and just on the right side, Rover Leader Captain E.W. Clarke.

On Monday 25 February 1935 Tring Council held a dinner party at the Rose and Crown Hotel. For Cllr John Bly there was a surprise presentation of a beautiful silver gilt chain and three-coloured enamel badge. The idea of presenting this to Mr Bly, and all succeeding chairmen, came from eighty-three-year-old Nathan Thompson who, with a few friends, provided the money for it. It was presented by his son-in-law, W.P. Milton, the manager of the Tring National Provincial Bank, as Mr Thompson was unable to attend. The chain and badge were designed free of charge by Tring jeweller and watchmaker, J.L. Clement, and made at cost. The wording 'Tring Urban District Council' was in raised letters on the badge surrounding the county emblem of a hart. Cllr Bly's name was inscribed on the centre link of the chain with many other links for future chairmen. Mr Bly was photographed wearing it a few months later at the Silver Jubilee celebrations. This impressive chain of office has been worn by chairmen and then mayors to this day.

On 6 May 1935 King George V and Queen Mary celebrated their Silver Jubilee. In Tring, a procession assembled in Duckmore Lane and went along the Western Road to the Robin Hood then back up the High Street, along Akeman Street to Tring Park. They were led by the Tring British Legion Band under bandmaster George Sayer, and followed by the 1st Tring Scout Troop with Mr N. Stenhouse, and then representatives of other organisations. The photograph shows the procession approaching the crossroads in the centre of Tring. On the left can be seen members of the council standing on a platform erected in front of the Market House. The weather was brilliant for the event and there were sports, decorated floats and other entertainment.

There was a competition for the best-decorated shops, houses and cottages. The prize for the best house was won by Mr E. Wright of Westcroft, Western Road. The award for the best-decorated cottage went to Mr Tugby of Miswell Lane. When the winner of the best shop was announced it was that of John Bly in the High Street but he felt that as chairman of the council he could not accept the prize and it went to the wool shop in the High Street. The photograph shows Cllr John Bly with his wife, who has just been presented with a bouquet of pink tulips by little Winnie Ferguson, of Ickneild Crescent, seen here. Mr and Mrs Bly are with the judges who were John Bagnall, Mr and Mrs A.T. Ives, Mrs F. Cox, Mrs E. Wright and Mr and Mrs S. Luck.

One of the features of the Jubilee day was a procession of decorated vehicles that made their way to the park where there was a panel of judges to choose the winners. Here one of the YMCA floats, 'Ten Men Went to Mow', is going up Akeman Street, where most of the houses had put out flags, many right across the road. The YMCA members who made up the team included Frank Johnson, Harold Brackley, Roland Rance, George Christopher, Fred Waterton, Wally Rance, Bert Wright and 'Knock' Higby with his dog.

Another group to enter floats in the procession was the Tring British Legion. Here on the right the women's branch had made theirs into a domestic scene entitled 'Women's Work is Never Done', something most of them probably knew only too well. Next to them the men's branch had turned one of Mr John Gower's coal lorries into an Army trench complete with sandbags and British 'Tommies' defending it. They won a prize for the most original tableau. The character standing in front is 'Old Bill' who featured in the First World War cartoons by Bruce Bairnsfather. Portraying him is Sam Marshall, the Secretary of the British Legion. In the centre at the back is Arthur Kitchener. To his right is Bill Dean and to his left D. Gunn. At the entrance to the trench stands Horace Bandy.

The children queued in the school playground to receive a souvenir mug presented to them by Lord Rothschild. The mugs were colourful with a portrait of the King and Queen surrounded by flags on the front and a coat of arms and the words 'Tring Jubilee Celebration' on the reverse.

After dark a bonfire on the downs was lit by Cllr John Bly. It had been carefully put together by the 1st Tring Scout Group under Scoutmaster Stenhouse. In the photograph the boys can be seen hauling wood up the hill a long way above the town.

When Cllr Bly lit the bonfire, a 'lighted taper' was rather roughly drawn in to indicate what he was doing. The evening's outdoor events ended with an illuminated procession which toured the town. The entrants were judged and the winner was Mrs R. Perkins with her replica of a floodlit Westminster Abbey. Earlier, Mrs Perkins had entered her model in the class for decorated prams. Finally a public dance was organised in the Victoria Hall by the British Legion and 300 people danced to the music of Roland Stevens and his band, some until two o'clock in the morning.

On August Bank Holiday Monday 1935 the Tring British Legion again held their annual fête, sports and carnival. An added attraction was a display by the Tring fire brigade in full fire-fighting uniform with their fire engine. They were led by Chief Fire Officer George Putnam and it was said they gave a very capable display giving evidence of good training, efficiency and enthusiasm.

As well as having a successful fête on August Bank Holiday the Tring British Legion arranged a New Year Treat at the Victoria Hall, inviting all children of Tring and New Mill aged between five and fourteen years. Each child was invited in person and about 450 of them accepted. The hall was decorated, paper hats were provided, the tables were laden with food and a programme of entertainment was arranged. The Legion Band played music, the Women's Glee Party sang songs, the children themselves recited poems and sang and two London conjurors came to mystify the audience. Just after eight o'clock each child went home with an apple, an orange, some sweets and a bar of chocolate. The photograph shows the children enjoying the fourth New Year Treat in 1936.

One building that was familiar to Tring people was the Tunnel Cement Works at Pitstone as many of them were employed there. Early in 1936 Mr L. Smith put in a planning application for the erection of a cement works. He called it Tunnel Cement as he had built an earlier cement works in West Thurrock in 1913 on the site of Tunnel Farm there, now a shopping complex. The first consignment of cement was delivered to Marley Tiles on 2 November 1937, just twenty months after planning consent was given. Four more chimneys were added and dominated the skyline for many years. The cement works closed in 1991 but it wasn't until 1999 that the site was cleared. The right to push the plunger to topple the chimneys was decided by raffle tickets which raised over £10,000 for local charities.

The Convent of St Francis de Sales and its school came to Tring from Margate in 1936. They settled in the house and grounds of Harvieston, in Aylesbury Road, built in 1902 for Dr James Brown, who had his surgery in the High Street. Later it was the home of Mrs Stenhouse. These photographs show the celebration in honour of Corpus Christi Day on the afternoon of Thursday 11 June 1936. A procession started at the door of the convent, shown here, and went through the grounds to an open-air altar. The banner of St Francis de Sales led the procession followed by Father W. Neville of Tring and the nuns and members of the Roman Catholic church. Here Father Neville and Father P. Graves of Berkhamsted are giving the benediction at the altar before the group returned to the convent. The convent remained a popular Tring school until the summer of 2000 when it was taken over by the Arts Educational School. It is now the St Francis De Sales Preparatory School, no longer a Roman Catholic school, but welcoming children of all denominations.

In April 1937 it was decided to convert some old buildings at the back of the Bell inn, in the High Street, into garages. When the front was removed these fine old beams were discovered and experts said they were thirteenth-century, so the find caused considerable interest. The old building was formerly the coach house for the mail coaches at the time when the inn was used as a mail house. The hayracks and food troughs for the horses can be seen on the right. The Bell inn is one of the oldest surviving public houses in Tring with written records going back to 1611. Today the old building is no longer in use but recent inspection shows that the wonderful old beams are still holding up the roof as they did centuries ago.

Two years after the Silver Jubilee, Tring was again in festive mood to celebrate the Coronation of King George VI and Queen Elizabeth on 12 May 1937. A similar photograph to that of 1935 shows the procession in the High Street, again led by the Tring British Legion, followed by schoolchildren. There were competitions for fancy dress, decorated cars, lorries, cycles and prams. A similar route was taken by the procession which this time started in Miswell Lane.

The women's section of the Tring British Legion entered two floats in the large tableaux class and won with their 'Gipsy Encampment', pictured here. Again there was a competition for the best decorated houses, cottages and shops. The winner of the 'house' class was the convent's Harvieston on the Aylesbury Road, an impressive building even before it was decorated.

The shops were judged by Lady Nairn and her daughter Mrs Sybil Clay, and they chose Arthur's as the winner. 'Arthur' was Arthur Gates whose family had the stationery and toy shop opposite on the corner of the High Street and Frogmore Street. Arthur started his hairdressing business in a back room there before moving to the little shop across the road. The theme of his window was 'The Crowning Glory' and depicted the coronation and the permanent wave for the ladies.

Following his success in the 1935 Jubilee class for decorated cottages John Tugby of 60 Miswell Lane again won a first prize in the same class at the Coronation celebrations. Here his display is photographed with him standing by his front door. The design of the Royal State Coach, pulled by three white horses and the other decorations show him to be a worthy winner.

All afternoon there was entertainment, including tightrope walking, acrobats and performing dogs from London. The programme of sports, with no entry fee, was open to all residents in the urban district. The slow bicycle race, pictured here, was probably a lot more difficult than it looked. There were children's teas in the Victoria Hall, with about 500 children in two relays, and tea for the old folk in the Church House and the Temperance Hall. At eight o'clock the broadcast of the King's Speech was heard through amplifiers in the park and an hour later there was a firework display.

Lord Lionel Walter Rothschild died on 27 August 1937. His last public appearance was when he presented Coronation gifts in May. His thick white beard made him look older than his sixty-nine years. Born in London on 8 February 1868, Lord Walter spent most of his life at Tring Park. He was an MP for mid-Bucks from 1899 until 1910 but his real passion was his museum, the first part of the building being a gift from his father on his twenty-first birthday. He was president of the Tring Conservative Association and the Tring Agricultural Association who put on the show in Tring Park each year. He had also been president of the Tring Park Cricket Club since 6 March 1885 – over fifty years! Lord Rothschild was buried at the Willesden Jewish Cemetery on Sunday 29 August.

After Lord Rothschild's death it was announced that he had bequeathed his private zoo and museum at Tring to the nation. The trustees at the British Museum discussed the offer at a meeting on 23 October. They said that the collection was of great scientific value, especially the butterflies and insects, but that grants would be needed from the government to maintain it. Meanwhile a dedicated team was continuing to run the museum headed by Dr Karl Jordan who had been with Lord Rothschild for more than forty years. The museum was taken over by the British Museum and has had a growing number of visitors over the years, especially after the decision no longer to charge entrance fees from December 2001.

A wedding that united two well-known Tring families took place in August 1937 when Dorothy Bagnall married George Prentice at Akeman Street Baptist church. The bridegroom's brother, Arthur, was the best man and the bridesmaids were Beryl Peck, a cousin of the bride, and Enid Badrick, a niece of the bridegroom.

Apart from his service in the RAF during the war George had a long career as a bus driver. He was popular with Tring commuters as, in all weathers, he drove the Tring to Aldbury bus via Tring station. This photograph shows George's bus at one end of his route by the pond in Aldbury.

This portrait, which hangs in the council offices, shows Cllr Ellis Houchen when he was chairman of Tring Urban District Council. He and Mr H.J. Gurney, the clerk, received the King's Coronation Medal from Buckingham Place in recognition of their services to the town. Mr Houchen had been re-elected to the Council in April 1937. He came to Tring from Cambridgeshire and lived in Miswell Lane. He retired from his drapery and hosiery business at the age of sixty and when he died in 1941 at the age of eighty he had been a councillor for twenty-six years.

These days George Bell's trip to America on the Queen Mary and his sixteen-day tour of the eastern states would not be thought of as remarkable, but in 1937, when he returned, the four pages that he wrote in the parish magazine aroused considerable interest. In January 1938 he was invited by the British Legion Women's Section to describe his time on what was described as 'Britain's wonder ship' and his journey of over 1,000 miles in seven different states. The picture of the ship would certainly give the impression that it was huge. Mr Bell produced a brochure account of his trip and the Cunard White Star Line, owners of the *Queen Mary*, ordered 10,000 copies of it.

George Bell was well known in Tring. He and his twin brother, Edward, were valued players in Tring Park Cricket Club, and he was a professional photographer, ensuring that he would return with a good record of his holiday. He said that America was too vast to describe adequately but added, 'I can only suggest that you save your pennies as we did and see the New World for yourself.' George Bell was the person who, with Frank Grace's slides and Frank's son Tom as 'lanternist', started the 'Old Tring' lantern lectures that were immensely popular, filling halls for many years. Later Tom's brother, Bob, replaced George.

For many years local people had enjoyed a wonderful day out when the Tring Show was held in Tring Park each year. Another popular annual event was the Tring British Legion's fête, also in Tring Park, on August Bank Holiday Monday. The Dagenham Girl Pipers, who had given a winter concert at the Victoria Hall about two years before, were chosen by the Legion to lead the procession to the fête in 1938. The photograph is taken in Akeman Street and the leader has just passed the butcher's shop, Dix and Sear, one of a number of small shops in the road. When they reached the park the girl pipers played their bagpipes at intervals during the afternoon and evening.

Tring Park Cricket Club has had an enviable record over the years for producing some very successful cricketers and memorable matches. On 10 May 1939 their Wednesday team played Hemel Hempstead at Tring. One of their star players was Albert Kempster. In 1936, playing for the Wednesday team and the First XI, he scored 1,249 runs and took 110 wickets in one season! Here he scored a brilliant 110 out of a total of 185 for 6 when Tring declared in time for tea. Hemel Hempstead played well but could only score 109 runs. Albert Kempster took three of their wickets for 32 runs. This photograph shows him going out to bat with fellow player Arthur Waldock. Against Hemel Hempstead Arthur took 3 for 14 and another bowler, Harry Mumford, took 3 for 25. The cricketers who played for the Wednesday team were often not free on a Saturday, many of them being shopkeepers.

The ninety-fifth and last one-day Tring Show was held on 10 August 1939. A month later the country was at war. After the war there were other shows in Tring Park but they were the Herts County Shows. In the 1939 show King George VI exhibited Suffolk horses and Red Poll cattle and Mrs Chamberlain, the wife of the prime minister, exhibited dogs. In this photograph little six-year-old Phyllis Killick is feeding one of the shire horses being shown by her father, Albert Killick, who was in charge of the horses at Home Farm in Park Road.

Congratulations were showered on Mr John Gower when he celebrated his ninety-fourth birthday on Sunday 3 November 1940. At the time he was living with his daughter and son-in-law in the Western Road but had only left his removals business, John Gower and Son, of Queen Street, about eighteen months before. He was thought to be the second oldest person in Tring, only a few months younger than Mrs John Brandon of Park Road. Mr Gower lived until 1945 when, at the age of ninety-nine years and five months he was found to have died peacefully in his rocking chair.

In 1940 Lord Beaverbrook, the Minister of Supply, made a nationwide appeal for aluminium to help the war effort. Cllr Hedges, reporting to the council, said that housewives all over the town had sacrificed perfectly good new things, that would be highly serviceable for years. It was said that people had brought in everything you could think of from vacuum cleaners to cake tins. Mr Wheeler, with his large outfitters business in the High Street, gave one window of his shop to display all the donations. A lot of the metal objects, and especially the beautiful gates to the mansion, were taken but found quite unsuitable and never used.

After a remarkable fifty years' devoted service to the Tring fire brigade, seventy-four-year-old Chief Officer George Putnam felt, in March 1940, that it was time for him to retire. He had been connected with the brigade since its formation in 1889 and, although at first rather reluctant to accept the promotion, he had been chief officer for the last twenty-eight years. Mr Putnam was the holder of the National Fire Brigade's Association silver medal for twenty years' service and qualified for six bars for each further five years' service. In recognition of his long service Chief Officer Putnam was given the rank of honorary captain of his old brigade and was presented with his uniform. This photograph shows Mr Putnam in front of his troop two years earlier when the chairman of the council presented long service medals to the firemen. Here he is decorating Second Officer William Welling, who also resigned in March 1940 after twenty-eight years' service. The firemen here are, from left to right: William Keele, Eddie Brackley, Harry Bull, George Hinton, Sid Lovell and William Welling. Just visible at the back are S. Harrop and Fred Rance.

Five

1941-1950

The Tring area was thought to be comparatively safe during the war and a large number of evacuees came from London and other places known to be at risk. In most cases Tring proved to be safe, but on the night of 30 January 1941 an enemy plane going home from a raid dropped a bomb on the village of Long Marston. The school was completely wrecked and the Boot public house opposite was severely damaged and had to be demolished. Amazingly the war memorial beside the school was left unscathed. Sadly the infant mistress, Mrs Whelan, was killed in the schoolhouse and a little girl evacuee suffered a broken leg. In the school magazine some time later thirteen-year-old Ronald Watt wrote, 'After the bomb dropped we did not go to school because there was nowhere to go.'

The local newspapers, when reporting the tragedy, were not permitted to name the village where the bomb had been dropped and described Long Marston as a 'tiny and secluded village in the Home Counties.' The photograph shows Mrs Whelan with the children from the school in fancy dress. The little clown on the left is Brian Walker and the girl at the front and the bigger girl to her left are June Chandler and Lavinia Chapman.

The Boot public house was damaged beyond repair in the bombing. Luckily the landlord and his wife, Mr and Mrs Alfred Frank Pearce, survived. It was said that the day afterwards Americans from the airbase at Marsworth came over with materials to do sufficient repairs to ensure that the bar could be opened in the evening. For nearly ten years the Boot carried on trading in a hut until in 1950 it was rebuilt. It is still very popular with local people. Mr and Mrs Pearce came to the Boot in 1934. Before that Mr Pearce had a very interesting career. He schooled polo ponies when he was employed by Captain Frank Rich, whose ponies were brought by well-known people, including Winston Churchill, who was a keen polo player in his younger days. Mr Pearce also taught riders to play polo and among his pupils he could name King George VI and the Duke of Windsor. Sadly he died in March 1950 just three weeks after the Boot had been rebuilt.

Following the success of War Weapons Week the previous year, it was decided to have a Warship Week in Tring in the third week in March 1942. The aim was to pay for at least part of a warship by people investing in National Savings. The ship chosen was an armed trawler HMS *Arctic Hunter*, the total cost of which would be £62,000. Tring Warship Week was officially opened by Air Vice Marshal MacEwen, air officer in command at Halton, Peggy Ashcroft, the actress, and Lady Davidson MP. A lot of events were arranged in Tring and the surrounding villages and by the end of the week £77,113 had been raised, more than enough to purchase the *Arctic Hunter*, pictured here.

On 31 March 1942 the Tring church clock 'celebrated' its sixtieth birthday. The casting for the clock face was made in 1882 by G. Grace and Son of Tring from a pre-carved wooden pattern. While work was in progress Mr Grace had reason to celebrate as his son, Gilbert Charles, was born on 17 March. A barrel of beer was set up at the foot of the scaffolding under the church tower so that all the workers could drink to the baby's health. The clock mechanism was regularly serviced by the High Street jewellers and watchmakers, J. Clement, who also cared for all the clocks at Lord Rothschild's mansion, so was usually most reliable. When in 1926 it did stop for a while it was at the time of the General Strike, prompting a reporter to state that, contrary to the spirit of the times, the clock in the tower of the parish church had refused to strike. It was soon repaired and chiming again.

In the spring of 1942 it was evident that more scrap metal was needed to help the war effort. A letter from H.J. Gurney, the clerk of the council, said that, before May, work would commence on the removal of railings in the entire urban district. Although claims for compensation were mentioned it was hoped that the railings would be given. An exception was made for those round the recreation ground, the safety of the children being considered more important.

By mid-May many iron railings had gone but later the Council expressed dissatisfaction with the way great sledgehammers had been used and damage done, and they regretted the loss of the beautiful gates to the Park. These gates, made in the workshops of G. Grace and Son, could, after a message was received from the Mansion, be opened and closed by one of Lord Rothschild's employees. Where these gates stood is now the entrance to Mansion Drive.

As can be seen from the war memorial, Tring did not lose as many of its young men in the Second World War as it had in the First. There were, of course, some families who suffered the tragic loss of a dearly loved husband, son or brother. This photograph shows Leonard William Howlett of the Sherwood Foresters Regiment, who was killed in action in North Africa in 1943 when only twenty years of age. Leonard was the only son of Mr and Mrs Harold Howlett whose hardware shop at 21-22 Charles Street was well known to local residents. Almost all his life Leonard attended the Akeman Street Baptist church where he had been a member of both the junior and senior choirs and a Sunday School teacher. He was a keen pigeon fancier and many people recall the pigeon lofts at the end of the Charles Street garden.

Early in 1943 the war had been going for more than three years and many families had not seen husbands, fathers or sons for some time. The BBC had been entertaining the troops with special programmes for them and arranged for messages to be broadcast to the servicemen. In March of that year eleven-year-old Rita Horne of Beaconsfield Road went with her mother, Louie Horne, to the BBC studio to broadcast a message to her father, Staff-Sergeant Sidney Horne who was serving in Madagascar. It was said that Rita, who was one of fifteen children sending a message to their fathers, spoke clearly with no nerves.

Two days later Staff-Sergeant Horne sent a telegram to his daughter to say that he had received her message loud and clear. During the war most servicemen had a photograph of themselves taken in uniform. Film for most people at home was not readily available and most of them could not use their cameras until after the war ended. This photograph of Rita, taken some time later, shows that the little girl who broadcast from the BBC grew up to be a very attractive young lady.

'Wings for Victory' week was in 1943. The target aimed for – £50,000 – was more than doubled and the £100,390 raised was enough to pay for a Sunderland flying boat. Part of a parade on 1 May were prams pushed by Tring mothers and led by Nurse Shore. A prize for the best baby, chosen by Lady Davidson MP, was given to Mr and Mrs George Prentice's little son, David George.

At the beginning of 1944 Mr and Mrs Arthur Crockett of Frogmore Street heard that their older son, Pte Arthur Raymond Crockett, had been missing since November of the year before. He had been in the Territorials before the war and was serving in the Middle East. Happily the next month Mr and Mrs Crockett received a postcard from him dated Christmas Day saying he was a prisoner of war in Germany and was safe and well. Pte Crockett returned to Tring and lived in the district all his life, always known as Ray. Young Ray is on the right side of the front row in this picture. Ray Crockett died in May 2001 at the age of eighty while on holiday with the British Legion in Belgium. The photograph shows, from left to right, back row: 'Stibby' Hallibone, Albert Bell, Danny Bartram. Front row: Eddie Russell, Dennis White, Ray Crockett.

The well-known Shakespearean actress and film star, Peggy Ashcroft, lived in Tring during the war while her husband was an officer in the Navy. She lived in the Rothschild's summer house at the top of the Oddy Hill, very little of which now remains. Peggy was always ready to help at local events. In March 1942 she opened Tring's Warship Week when over £77,000 was raised in National Savings bonds. The next year she participated in a sale in aid of the Red Cross in the cattle market where livestock was sold and over £1,000 was raised. In May 1944 in Tring's Salute the Soldier week she was given a silver key to open the selling centre at Wheeler Brothers' shop in the High Street. In her speech Peggy said she was glad to have qualified to be a member of that exclusive society the towns 'people of Tring'. That year the target of £50,000 was raised to the grand total of £121,564, a magnificent effort by the patriotic townspeople.

Toward the end of 1944, when the war was progressing well in Europe, it was decided that the Home Guard was no longer needed in Tring and in December there was a standing down parade on the drive in front of the Mansion. Two of the older Home Guardsmen ceremoniously handed in their rifles to two young Army cadets. This photograph shows some very well-known Tring people, ARP Warden Robert Hedges, whose shop, now called by its present owners the Old Stables, is still trading at the bottom of Miswell Lane, and Sgt Harry Bone of the Home Guard, whose general store halfway up Miswell Lane was carried on by his son Mervyn and his wife until quite recently. Mervyn, seen here with his toy rifle, was three years old at the time.

In 1944 a heartbreaking event took place that fortunately had a happy ending. In April the sisters and brother of Pte James Wood of 8 Westwood Lane, Tring, received the news that he had died of wounds in the Far East, on 17 March. Pte Wood enlisted in the Territorials before the war and by 1942 he was in Ceylon. At the time of his 'death' he was twenty-four. In June of the same year his family received a letter from him, dated 5 May, saying that he had been wounded in the leg, and a second letter, dated 6 May, said that he was convalescing. The family wrote to their MP Lady Davidson who contacted the War Office and confirmed that enquiries were being made. They at last received an apology and confirmation that Pte Jimmy Wood was in fact alive and well. Two years after the war he married Elsie May Bradding at Tring parish church and the heading of a report in the local paper simply said 'Reported Dead – Now Wed'.

In August 1944 the Herts Athletic Championships were held at Watford and Mr Jimmy Attryde from Wigginton came second in the Herts County one-mile championship in a time of 4 minutes 47 seconds. The winner was an international runner, E.J. Nankivell. The next month Jimmy won the five-mile race at the Newport Pagnell Show in 26 minutes having taken the lead in the third mile. He was 300 yards in front of the second man. Jimmy was then a member of the Finchley Harriers. He went on to have numerous other successes. He was a reporter and sports editor with the *Bucks Herald* newspaper during the war and afterwards and was a familiar figure in Tring researching information for his columns. Jimmy married Joan Smith of Hill Green Farm, Wigginton, in June 1949 and lived in the area all his long life. He died at his home on 28 July 2001.

In spite of the difficulties during the war caused by the young men and women joining the services, many young Tring girls did get married, even if clothes rationing meant they couldn't have a white wedding. In the last years of the war there were a large number of 'GI brides' who later sailed to America. The US airmen were stationed at Marsworth. Local girls had also joined the services and here at their wedding at Tring parish church in March 1944, Irene Jones, now known as 'Janie', was in the WRNS and the groom, Frank Standen from London, was in the RAF air-sea rescue service. Before joining the services Irene was a Cubmaster with the 1st New Mill Cubs who formed a guard of honour as the couple left the church, when the bride was presented with a lucky horseshoe. The bells were then rung at the church where the bride's grandfather, Frederick James Reeve, had been captain of the bell-ringers for over twenty-seven years.

This wedding, although not taking place in Tring, was of considerable interest to Tring people as both the groom and the best man were well known locally. The charming bride was Joan Griffith of Hemel Hempstead and the groom was Arthur Kitchener, a member of the Tring police force. His best man was his younger brother, Ron, seen here in uniform when he was serving as a sergeant in the Guards. Both young Kitcheners, now retired, had successful careers, Arthur gaining promotion in the police service and Ron having the insurance business in the High Street that still bears his name. He is also well known for his enthusiasm for Tring's local history.

Early in 1945 news reached Pte Doug Reeve's parents in Akeman Street that he had been wounded in Burma serving with the Northampton Regiment. This early photograph shows him as a boy on a Sunday School outing to Tring Park from the Akeman Street Baptist church with Mrs D.M. Bagnall. The boys are, from left to right, back row: Victor Harris, Bill Wright, Doug Reeve. Front row: Roy Dartnell, Lionel Harris, Len Wright.

Doug was born in Tring and spent his boyhood there, joining the 2nd Battalion Herts Territorials in March 1939. He was called up on 1 December that year and, after training in England and some time guarding our coasts, he went to India and on to Ceylon for jungle training. He then went on to Burma, helping to retake the country after the British forces had had to retreat some time before. Doug served throughout the war with Pte Jimmy Wood who was reported killed in 1944 and it was he who first wrote to inform Jimmy's family in Westwood Lane that their brother was still alive. Happily Doug survived the war and returned to Tring where he still lives with his wife, Dena, in Akeman Street.

This photograph shows one of Tring's best-known inhabitants, Bob Grace, in a less familiar role, serving in the Army in Ranchi, India, in 1945, where his early interest and expertise with radio was put to good use in the war effort. Bob came from generations of Graces who ran the mill in Akeman Street, now private houses and named 'Graces Maltings'. He served on Tring Council for about thirty years, working to preserve the countryside and aspects of Tring he knew so well. His most popular role in the town was that of historian and his 'Old Tring' lantern lectures were sure to draw large crowds wherever they were given. He was accompanied first by his brother, Tom, as 'lanternist' and later by his niece, Nuala. All those interested in Tring's history have reason to be grateful to Bob Grace.

Mrs Sarah Reed was one of Tring's oldest inhabitants when she died at her home, 29 Park Road, on 13 September 1945, at the age of almost ninety-three. She was born Sarah Matthews at Buckland Common and as a girl she was a straw plaiter. She would come to Tring market with her mother to sell straw-plait. When she grew older she worked at two local vicarages as a nursemaid, one at St Leonards and one at Wigginton. She married the postman Henry Alfred Reed on 6 June 1876 and came to live in Tring where she stayed for the rest of her life. She had been a widow for thirteen years. She and Henry had five children: one son, Eric, the well-known Tring blacksmith, and four daughters, Laura, Alice, Hilda and Ethel.

On Wednesday 12 June 1946, Flt Lt R.J. Kilby's shire stud had a very successful day at the Essex Agricultural Show. Mr and Mrs Kilby entered four horses and by the end of the day they won ten awards including two championships and two reserve championships. His horses were a gelding, Birkwood Grey Duke, a two-year-old filly, Kytes Mayflower, and a yearling filly, Kytes Grey Star. Another two-year-old filly, Mrs Kilby's Beech House Pearl, was second and reserve champion to her husband's Kytes Mayflower. In charge of these beautiful horses at Home Farm in Park Road was Albert Killick, seen here with one of his champions.

For the Tapping family, 6 December 1946 was a very special day. On that day Mr and Mrs Walter Tapping of 42 Dundale Road celebrated their golden wedding and one of their grandchildren, Vera Crockett, celebrated her twenty-first birthday. A party was held at Mr and Mrs Tapping's home with two cakes, one with fifty candles, the other twenty-one. Mr Tapping, a retired postman born in Princes Risborough, came to Tring in 1910. His wife, née Sarah Ann Williams, came from London. They had seven sons, all of whom served in the war, and three daughters. Their grand-daughter, Vera, is well known in Tring as Mrs McKernan, as she and her late husband 'Mac' were on the staff of the Tring Museum. Mr and Mrs Tapping are seen here outside their home with their family. From left to right, back row, standing: Walter Harrison, Ray Crockett, Cecil Tapping, Roland Tapping, Betty Tapping, Vera Danby, Harry Danby, Miss Danby, Mr Danby Jnr, May Tapping, Frank Crockett, Alex Tapping, Gladys Crockett, Reg Tapping, Logan Tapping. Front row: Amy Tapping, Kath Crockett, Albert Tapping with Ann, Mary Tapping, Connie Tapping, Walter and Sarah Tapping, Vera Crockett with Esther Tapping, Joyce O'Leary, Daphne Tapping, Norman Tapping, Peter Tapping.

A trophy came to Tring on Saturday 24 May 1947 when Tring Town Football Club beat Bovingdon in the final of the West Herts Minor Cup at Apsley. The last time the trophy came to Tring was in 1921 when it was won by the YMCA team. It was an exciting match as in the first half Tring were ahead with goals scored by Alan Ball and Derek Allen. In the second half Bovingdon rallied and scored two goals to equalise. From the start of extra time Tring again dominated and another goal by Derek Allen and one by Reg Mills meant that Tring won 4-2. The winning team was, from left to right, back row: Frank Butler, Fred Patterson, W. Mills, Ken Dwight, Derek Allen, Gary Harrop. Front row: Alan Ball, Cyril Price, Roy Waterton, Reg Mills, Charlie Cummings.

In 1947 Tring lost one of its best-known personalities, John Woodman of Longfield Road. When he died at the age of eighty-seven he was described as 'an encyclopaedia of long-ago local affairs'. His father had been landlord at the Plough inn and the Green Man, both in the Lower High Street. Mr Woodman spent most of his working life as a carpenter on the Tring Park Estate. When he was born there, the Williams family rented the estate. This photograph shows him with his wife, who died in 1940, his three daughters and two sons. At the back are Lilian the eldest daughter, Eric the elder son and the middle daughter Nellie. At the front are Winifred and Leonard, the youngest children.

Standing under the familiar arch at the entrance to Tring parish church are Mr and Mrs Ron Wheeler after their wedding in April 1947. Ron was well known in Tring as his family had the drapers and outfitters in the High Street just beyond the church. His bride, Aline, who came from London and served with the WAAF during the war, soon became known as a talented artist. Specialising in oil paintings of the countryside surrounding the town, she had several successful local exhibitions. One of Aline's paintings hangs in a prominent position in Tring Public Library. She was also a popular art teacher at the Arts Educational School in Tring Park.

As early as 1944 the council discussed the building of new homes for the returning servicemen. They decided to buy 6.7 acres of woodland near the junction of Park Road and Duckmore Lane. A lot of people did not approve of their choice and the chairman said he had about 400 signatures from people against the choice of the site. There were, however, a lot of others who thought it was ideally situated for the schools, shops, surgeries etc., and the land was purchased for £812. While the houses were being built in 1947, Britain had one of the worst winters in living memory with a lot of snow and power cuts, making it difficult for those in the building trade, but by the end of the year several houses were ready for occupation. The council found it almost impossible to please everybody when it came to allocating the new houses. One disappointed ex-serviceman wrote that he had six children from six months to eighteen years packed into one bedroom like sardines and he had no gas, water or electricity. Later more council houses were built in various parts of the town. Many Woodland Close homes have now been bought by their tenants. Although plain in appearance they were well built, with three bedrooms, a bathroom, reasonable-sized rooms and garden, something not enjoyed by many of the servicemen in pre-war days.

The reservoirs have always been popular with fishermen. In August 1947 a huge fish was found floating in the water. It was 5ft 6in long and although partly disintegrated still weighed 46lb. It was a continental catfish introduced by Lord Rothschild at the start of the century as an experiment. It must have survived well but it was the first time one had been seen.

The family of Mr and Mrs Fred Harrop of 12 Henry Street, Tring. They had seven sons and four daughters. The second son, Fred, is absent from this group; he had emigrated to Australia and the photograph was taken to send to him. Mr and Mrs Harrop were married in 1898 at Tring parish church and they celebrated their golden wedding on 8 October 1948 when he was seventy-three and she seventy-four years old. By 1948 they had thirteen grandchildren. This picture taken some ten years earlier shows, from left to right, back row: Les, Stan, Garry, Bill, George, Jim. Front row: Kath, Hilda, Mr and Mrs Harrop, Eve, Mary.

On 21 January 1949 the bells of Tring parish church were rung to celebrate the golden wedding of Mr and Mrs Frederick James Reeve of 58 Dundale Road. Mrs Reeve was Mary Ann Fitkin before her marriage and both were life-long residents of Tring. They were married at Tring church by the late Revd S.W. Tidswell. Mr Reeve had been busy all his life. He was employed by the late Frederick Butcher and Arthur Butcher as a gardener and later as head gardener for a total of forty-eight years. He was also a member of Tring fire brigade for twenty-three years and a caretaker of the fire station for seventeen years. During the First World War he was a special constable and a member of the St John Ambulance brigade. On the day of their golden wedding, when Mr and Mrs Reeve were seventy-six and seventy-five respectively, there was a family gathering at their home which included two children, five grandchildren and one great-grandchild.

In 1949 it was decided by Tring Council to have a permanent memorial to the young men who had died in the Second World War. Their names were added to the memorial in front of the church but it was thought that a garden of rest made in their memory could be enjoyed by all the people of Tring. The site chosen was that of Lord Rothschild's water garden, by then neglected and overgrown. In December Cllr Robert Grace announced that the transfer of land was being arranged with Lord Rothschild's agent. It was nearly a year before the legal procedures were completed and in the following September it was announced that work was about to start on the memorial garden. The photograph shows the lily pond when it was cared for by Lord Rothschild's gardeners.

In January 1949 the New Mill Dramatic Club had a big hit with their pantomime *Cinderella*, produced and directed by Miss Joan Luxton. Here members of the cast pose for a photograph. From left to right, back row: Rosemary Hillyard, Kathleen Nutkins, Valerie Seymour, -?-. Front row: Peggy Warwick (Prince Charming), -?-, Ann Fulks, Pat Dwight, June Drake, Vanda Badrick, Mary Perkins (Cinderella), Brenda Drake, -?-, Jane Cowan, -?-, -?-.

One wonders what other events were planned for Easter Monday, 10 April 1950. As can be seen from this photograph the weather was wet and windy and far from ideal when Rose Hooper of Tring station married Douglas Sinclair, also from Tring, at the parish church on that day. The vicar, the Revd T.K. Lowdell, conducted the service and the five bridesmaids were June and Grace Hooper, the bride's twin sisters, Eileen Hooper, another sister of the bride, Margaret Halliday, the bridegroom's cousin, and Barbara Wright, a friend of the bride. The page boy was Raymond Hooper, the bride's brother, and the best man was Gerald Boniface. Doug served in the Army but perhaps was best known in Tring as a member of the local ambulance service and the Tring fire brigade. Both were prominent members of the British Legion; Rose was on the committee of the women's section. They have had a long and happy marriage, celebrating their golden wedding with their children and grandchildren in April 2000.

By 1950 the owner of Home Farm, shown here from the side, was Mr John Schroeder who had bought it two years before from Flt Lt Kilby. Mr Kilby had moved his shire horses to a new home at Buckland Common. No one in Tring seems able to remember Mr Schroeder but it would appear that he and his family lived in the house for a short time. When it was announced at the beginning of 1950 that the Moss family from Bray in Berkshire were taking over Home Farm, renaming it White Cloud Farm, it was Alfred Moss and his wife, Aileen, who then had a reputation in the motor racing world. Mr Moss had raced at Brooklands and in America he had competed in dirt-track racing at Indianapolis. Mr and Mrs Moss's son, Stirling, had started on his racing career and already had several wins but at that time was yet to have the successes that made him, arguably, the most famous racing driver of all time.

This photograph shows the yard at Home Farm after Flt Lt Kilby had added a decorative fish pond with life-size female figures at the corners.

In September 1950, on the day before his twenty-first birthday, Stirling Moss beat Britain's top racing drivers to win the RAC Tourist Trophy event in Belfast, driving a Jaguar. The papers still called him 'Stirling Moss of Tring'. He ended the year with a remarkable result in France when, with his co-driver, Ken Gregory, he broke thirteen records held previously by French and Italian drivers. Driving a Keift car they broke records at distances ranging from 50 kilometres to 200 miles. Back home he was awarded the British Racing Drivers Gold Star for road racing and the Richard Seaman Trophy for the British driver gaining the most marks in foreign racing. Stirling's fifteen-year-old sister, Pat, was at the time one of the country's most successful junior show jumpers. She had continued success in adult jumping, especially with her brilliant horse, Danny Boy, and later concentrated on rally driving, being Ladies European Champion for six years.

White Cloud House is still a home but the farm buildings have now been converted into a complex of private homes and the name Home Farm has been reinstated.

In 1905 plans had been passed for Lord Nathaniel Rothschild to build a bothy in Tring Park Gardens. As this old photograph, taken soon after it was built, shows, it was quite an impressive building, but there were a large number of gardeners employed on the Tring Park Estate. After Lord Walter Rothschild died in 1937 the estate was split up and sold and the disused bothy began to suffer from neglect..

Towards the end of 1950 an Edgware firm making plastics applied to Tring Council for permission to convert the Rothschilds' bothy in London Road into a small factory. The local planning authority opposed the idea because of the awkward bend in the road and the fact that the memorial gardens were to be made nearby. Tring councillors disagreed as the bothy had been derelict for six years and jobs were needed in the town. Their opinions were obviously heeded as William Cox Ltd took over the bothy and extended the buildings. Some of the plastic goods made there included Belisha beacons, television screens, roof-lights and roadworks cones and they provided employment for Tring people for many years. The picture shows the bothy while Cox's were there. It is now the site of Tring's Tesco superstore.